Absolute Essentials of International Business

As challenges to the era of globalisation emerge, international business grows in importance and complexity as a field of study. This shortform textbook introduces learners to the frameworks within which international business occurs and to the range of actions that companies might undertake in these environments.

Owing to an emphasis on cross-border interactions, international business is a politicised field, and this book provides readers with the tools to deepen their understanding not only of the actions that companies might take but also of the economic, societal, cultural and political frameworks affecting how decisions are made.

With a refreshing realism in its approach, this book will be perfect brief reading for students required to understand the obstacles that global business practitioners must overcome to succeed.

Alan Sitkin is Senior Lecturer in International Business and Sustainability at Regent's University London. He recently served eight years in London Borough of Enfield as Councillor and Cabinet Member for Economic Regeneration. This followed a previous 15-year career in International Finance working out of Paris, Zurich and London.

Karine Mangion-Thornley is a Senior Lecturer in International Business and Human Resources at Regent's University London, a PhD Candidate at Oxford Brookes University, UK and a Researcher at the Institute of Coaching, McLean/Harvard Medical School, USA. She holds a 10-year experience in talent and leadership development in global organisations as consultant, coach and guest speaker.

Absolute Essentials of Business and Economics

Textbooks are an extraordinarily useful tool for students and teachers, as demonstrated by their continued use in the classroom and online. Successful textbooks run into multiple editions, and in endeavouring to keep up with developments in the field, it can be difficult to avoid increasing length and complexity.

This series of shortform textbooks offers a range of books which zero-in on the absolute essentials. In focusing on only the core elements of each sub-discipline, the books provide a useful alternative or supplement to traditional textbooks.

Titles in this series include:

Absolute Essentials of Green Business
Alan Sitkin

Absolute Essentials of International Business
Alan Sitkin and Karine Mangion-Thornley

Absolute Essentials of Project Management
Paul Roberts

Absolute Essentials of Business Behavioural Ethics
Nina Seppala

Absolute Essentials of Corporate Governance
Stephen Bloomfield

Absolute Essentials of Business Ethics
Peter A. Stanwick and Sarah D. Stanwick

For more information about this series, please visit: www.routledge.com/Absolute-Essentials-of-Business-and-Economics/book-series/ABSOLUTE

Absolute Essentials of International Business

Alan Sitkin and
Karine Mangion-Thornley

Routledge
Taylor & Francis Group

LONDON AND NEW YORK

First published 2021
by Routledge
2 Park Square, Milton Park, Abingdon, Oxon OX14 4RN

and by Routledge
605 Third Avenue, New York, NY 10017

Routledge is an imprint of the Taylor & Francis Group, an informa business

Copyright © 2021 Alan Sitkin and Karine Mangion-Thornley

British Library Cataloguing-in-Publication Data
A catalogue record for this book is available from the British Library

Library of Congress Cataloging-in-Publication Data
A catalog record has been requested for this book

ISBN 13: 978-0-367-07710-5 (hbk)

Typeset in Bembo
by codeMantra

For Raphael, Nina and Candice

To L, D, J, L and E, from V and me. sf one and all

Contents

Acknowledgements

It is impossible to pay tribute to everyone who has contributed to my internationalism – being the second defining attribute of my life (after the love shared with family, friends and indeed strangers).

At a personal level, it started with the *Quinto Lingo* magazines that Dad and Mom kindly got for me as a kid, alongside the Spanish lessons and Wilshire Blvd Academy – all awakening me to the rich possibilities of a world beyond our home shores. I then became my high school's first student to ever study three languages and thank Francis Waas RIP for his Europhilia. Then came the UCSB junior year abroad: dear Cathy Domecq and the Bearnais; Andy, Gary and Catherine introducing me to Bordeaux; Richard, Remi, Yannick, Phillippe making me feel at home there – and the die was cast. I would spend my life as a stranger in strange lands.

Thank you to my darling Verena for teaching me that Europe isn't only France but also Hamburg and more. Thank you to Parisian Lea and Zuricher Dani for deepening my Continental roots; to Jo, Leo and Ellis for my English blood; and to Jim, Sue and Roger for letting me have my cake and eat it too.

At a professional level, thank you to AJ Fritz & Co; to IEP and HEC; to the four banks (and especially their customers) for letting me experience a bona fide international business career; to Transalver Ltd's French clients; and to Regents University London for its colleagues (including Nick Bowen and now Karine) and students coming from all over the world. Thank you also to Routledge's Terry Clague and to our wonderful artist Marie Dubois, for your friendly help in making this book a reality.

Lastly, by definition being an internationalist means belonging to a community defined by values rather than nationality. So I'd like to finish by acknowledging some of the many instances of true internationalism that I've witnessed, and which have bolstered my own beliefs.

These include Achilleas and Ahmet's embodiment of Cypriot reconciliation; cousin Josh for his upbringing and own marriage; the UK Remain campaign; and everyone evolved enough to understand that a smart and moral life builds bridges not walls. Thank you one and all for fighting the good fight.

Alan Sitkin

Food. In my family, we talk constantly about food. In good times, in bad times; at a distance or around the table.

Food. Keeps us grounded and connected as we live in different countries.

Food. For sharing and discovering, during both the highs and lows.

International Business is food to me, a continuous blend of creativity, experience and insights across borders. So, I am grateful for the cultural smorgasbord brought by my husband, parents, grandparents, brothers and their families, "The Best" dance sisters, and friends.

Thank you to Nick Bowen and Alan Sitkin, who welcomed me to the International Business table at Regent's University London. And also, to the students and colleagues who make international encounters an invigorating diet.

A special thank you to those who thought that writing a book whilst completing a PhD was pure madness, but still supported me in this endeavour (and, they were right!).

Thank you to Terry Clague from Routledge for sharing recipes, songs, books and fruitful advice and to Marie Dubois who so well captured our views in her drawings.

I hope you will enjoy the result of this stimulating concoction. So, thank you for reading.

Bon appétit!

Karine Mangion-Thornley

Foreword

For thousands of years, trade has been a key driver of social and economic progress in most if not all countries worldwide. Through trade, people have been able to access ideas, technologies, best practices, goods and services that were less available in their homeland – while earning good money selling their own output abroad. It is also because of trade that billions of individuals were able, over the past few decades alone, to overcome conditions of abject poverty. Lastly and probably as importantly, international business teaches everyone on Planet Earth an initial fundamental value, namely that what separates us from one another – the language we speak, how we look, the country that claims us as a citizen – is infinitely less important than our common humanity.

Yet despite these manifest virtues, recent years have witnessed the resurgence of parochial nationalism based on a counterfactual blaming of "the other" for any and all of the problems that humans face as part of their normal lives. Now, it is true that certain aspects of globalisation will have harmed certain populations in certain ways, largely because they neglected the absolute imperative that trade provide reciprocal benefits and not lead to exploitation or inequality. The reality, however, is that many mechanisms exist to remedy international business practices' few potentially negative effects – making demagogues' rejection of trade's manifold benefits all the more self-harming hence unintelligent.

The COVID-19 crisis that erupted at the dawn of the 2020s serves as a further reminder of the need for a more rational analysis of the macro- and micro-level contours of international business. A few voices have claimed that the crisis requires the abandonment of trade because disease can be transmitted across borders. This is nonsensical, however: the virus was transmitted by humans, not the exchange of goods and services; lockdowns have damaged domestic supply chains as much if not more than many international ones; and the wealth creation that trade enables will be sorely needed in the years to come as the world tries to cope with the economic devastation that COVID-19 is also causing.

Of course, it is highly probable that international business will shift forms after a crisis of this magnitude – much as it has adapted over the course of thousands of years to the many sea changes characterising the history of out civilisations. Moreover, it is this ongoing flux that makes international business such an interesting and dynamic discipline, one can only be accurately taught and learnt by practitioners willing to embrace diversity and capable of calculating the potential organisational implications for business.

The authors have adopted a flexible and variegated worldview in writing this book: because it corresponds to their own experience; and because of their conviction that there is no one best way to practice international business. Chapter 1 starts with this principle. Readers are heartily encouraged to debate it – like everything else in this book. Because the second fundamental value that international business embodies is the freedom to debate. And to enjoy debating.

To trade or not to trade – that is the question.

1 Introduction

The simplest definition for international business is "cross-border economic activity". It is a type of enterprise that has existed in various forms ever since different human populations first began trading items of value many thousands of years ago. Nowadays, the term refers not only to physical goods but also to services, capital, technology and human resources. The first point to make about this discipline is that it covers a very broad range of endeavours that have evolved hugely over time – explaining why historical analysis is so relevant to international business studies.

The second point to make is that some aspects of domestic business also apply in international business but are treated differently. Similarly, international business covers most if not all of the same topics as international management – but goes much further. Where international management focuses largely on individuals operating within a corporate setting, international business also incorporates the broader political, economic, social, technological, philosophical and environmental contexts within which companies operate. Indeed, it is this focus on the interactions between "macro" and "micro" level aspects that gives international business its distinctive philosophy and enduring attraction.

Philosophy and preliminary concepts

International business raises specific challenges that practitioners and academics ignore at their peril. Companies or individuals leaving a "home country" with which they are familiar can find it very difficult to adjust to a "host country" where the people and environment are foreign to them. There is no doubt that the process of globalisation has caused the world to shrink in recent years so that international differences are no longer as consequential as they once were. At the same time, it is unrealistic and even dangerous to assume that societies worldwide are converging to such an extent that there is no longer any need to study their economic, political and cultural differences (Chapter 3). The recognition that the world remains a complex and diverse place is best expressed through the distinction made between the terms "global" and "international".

"Globalisation" is associated with the idea of a single world and therefore stresses similarities between communities, hence greater cosmopolitanism and tolerance for diversity. "International" business, on the other hand, starts by emphasising areas of divergence. There is a strong argument that this latter approach is more useful to learners since it respects the obstacles that practitioners will actually face. One such obstacle is the retreat to narrow nationalism and even xenophobia that is exemplified in certain recent political developments. Another is the ongoing perception that international business exacerbates inequality by benefiting certain constituencies while harming others (Chapter 4). The trend towards closer cross-border business relations is strong but not irreversible – learners will therefore benefit most if international business is taught in a way that helps them consider strategies for overcoming the market entry barriers they are highly likely to face during their careers (Chapter 6). This is complicated because strategies and behaviour that apply in one situation are often of little or no relevance in another. Hence this book's central philosophy that helping learners develop a flexible mindset is more empowering than imparting any sense that there is just "one best way" of doing international business.

Companies and international business

Although individual enterprise does constitute one component of international business, the vast majority of the actions comprising this field are undertaken by companies, ranging from huge firms to small and medium-sized enterprises (SMEs) and even micro-firms that may be "born global" from the very outset.

The general terminology that this book uses to refer to companies with dealings outside of their home market is "multinational enterprises" MNEs. Other books may make reference to "multinational corporations" (MNC), "transnational corporations" (TNC) or global firms. Each of these terms designates a specific kind of company, however. MNE is a more neutral term and therefore preferable.

MNE configurations

A firm that operates facilities in one single country but trades outside of its borders qualifies as an MNE. So does a firm whose configuration involves headquarters in one country and subsidiaries established elsewhere through foreign direct investment (FDI), which is when an MNE takes a stake in an operation physically located in a foreign country. These two activities – trade and FDI – are the main pillars of international business.

One of the most noteworthy strategies pursued by many MNEs in recent decades has involved having each of their subsidiaries worldwide specialise in a specific functional activity, reflecting the competitive advantages of the place where it is operating. The net effect of this management paradigm – a corporate implementation of the international division of labour principles that Adam Smith's classical trade theory first applied to countries (Chapter 2) – is that international business today increasingly involves trade between an MNE's different international subsidiaries and/ or with its foreign suppliers or vendors. Hence the importance of understanding how MNEs organise their relational networks, including the talents they nurture (Chapter 11) to keep up with the changes happening in the many different markets where they operate.

International value chains

The most useful way of picturing MNEs' work organisation is to envision the production and sale of a good or service as a series of acts that each add to an item's value when it is transformed from raw material to a semi-processed module before ending up as a finished product (see Figure 1.1). This succession of activities is called the value chain and can broadly be broken down between production-related upstream (Chapter 8) and marketing-related downstream (Chapter 9) operations – without forgetting the specifically international financial management in which all MNEs engage (Chapter 10). One of the main features of international business today is that many firms do not perform by themselves all the activities comprising their value chain but instead outsource one or several stages to external counterparts. This applies particularly to MNEs in sectors like computing (e.g. Apple, Dell) or automobiles (e.g. Toyota, Volkswagen) where the main production activity involves assembling parts that are acquired from suppliers and not manufactured by the company itself (Chapter 7).

As a result, it could be more accurate to represent an international value chain as the sum of several intermediary value chains. But because value accrues more rapidly in some activities than in others – reflecting unequal "terms of trade" – another fundamental question in international business is "who does what where". This is particularly important given that many of the strategic actions taken by MNEs (and countries) are specifically intended to improve their terms of trade.

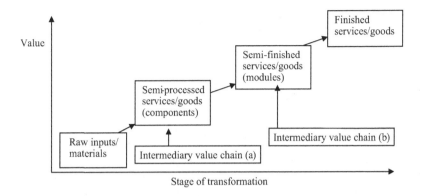

Figure 1.1 International value chains: who does what where.

A theoretical discipline rooted in empirical realities

International business is also a living subject, rooted in the relationship between concepts and actions. For this reason, it is crucial that practitioners and students develop the ability to analyse the basic concepts of the discipline in terms of real-world developments.

Evidence for the topicality of international business can be seen, for instance, in the way trade volumes had skyrocketed over recent decades, increasing much more rapidly than total global gross domestic product (GDP) at least, until the COVID-19 pandemic. This means that international business accounts today for a much higher percentage of total economic activity than it used to. Just one generation ago, the sum total of imports plus exports accounted for around 10% of the US gross domestic product (GDP); 25% to 30% of GDP in medium-sized industrial nations like Germany, France and Japan; and around 50% of GDP in smaller open economies like the Netherlands. Today these percentages have risen dramatically, usually by a factor of two or more. This has not only happened in the world's older industrialised countries (the Global North) but also and especially in emerging Global South economies like China and India, which seem every year to host a higher percentage of the headquarters of the MNEs found in *Fortune* magazine's famous top Global 500 list (see Figure 1.2).

Of course, different explanations exist for the ascendance of international business. At a very basic level of analysis, one leading factor has been the efficiency advantage many economic interests derive from business activities being organised internationally rather than domestically. A major example is the inflation-reducing effects of China

	Number of Fortune 500 MNE headquarters (2019)	Number of Fortune 500 MNE headquarters (2005)
China (with Taiwan)	129	16
USA	121	176
Japan	52	81
France	31	37
Germany	29	39
UK	17	35
South Korean	16	11

Figure 1.2 Changing geography of *Fortune* Global 500 multinational headquarters.

becoming a global manufacturing power – consumers worldwide benefit from low-cost Chinese imports, leaving these populations with more disposable income to spend on other goods. At the same time, international business has enabled hundreds of millions of Chinese households to climb out of abject poverty. This is an exciting market opportunity for producers from both the Global North and Global South (see Chapter 12) – a development that is incontrovertibly positive, for both business and ethical reasons.

Of course, there is no doubt that the displacement of production activities resulting from this trend has had a negative effect on those employment basins that have lost economic functions they used to enjoy, and which are understandably unhappy with this turn of events – explaining why politics is always crucial to international business studies. The question then becomes if these constituencies are right to blame trade disruption for the very real problems they have faced or if – as per research by both the Organisation for Economic Cooperation and Development (OECD) and the Centre for European Reform – domestic policies (particularly redistributive failures) and technological change bear greater responsibility for rising income inequality. The present book very much supports this latter view.

The drivers of international business

Because it is human beings who formulate MNEs' micro-level responses to the macro-level circumstances they face, there is necessarily a subjective component in the international business decisions they make. This subjectivity is rooted in managers' personal psychology, and in the paradigms shaping their worldview at a given moment in time. Deconstructing the subjective reasons underlying a decision is often very useful, particularly to advanced learners. Having said that, as in other disciplines, international business strategy tends to be an easier way of understanding thinking in this field.

Internal drivers

Expanding sales

The vast majority of MNEs throughout history have started in their home markets before deciding to move abroad because they saw an advantage in doing so. Once a firm has built a system allowing it to produce and market a product or service efficiently, it may wish to leverage the competencies it has developed by selling the finished good, with or without adaptation, into a new market. Thus, on the downstream side, expanding sales is the main driver of international business. This is especially true when a company is looking to move into a foreign country that seems more accessible because of its perceived political, economic and/or cultural similarities. The hope here is that the MNE will be able to seamlessly transplant the sales skills developed in one country to another.

There are also strategic reasons why companies increasingly organise their commercial efforts to embrace international markets as a matter of course. As mentioned above, one basic principle of modern production is that making and selling large volumes is beneficial because it creates economies of scale. In a similar vein, the more experience a company acquires in making something, the more productive it gets in doing so. As a result, many companies want to size their production operations to achieve a critical mass. To justify these investments and avoid surplus capacities, they must often sell more than if they were simply serving domestic customers. This is especially true if the firm comes from a small country.

Of course, the best outcome for a company is when customer preferences in a foreign market that it is entering resemble the demands it faces at home. In this case, the company can standardise its products and achieve economies of scale by simply selling more of the same thing abroad. In many markets, however, consumer demands may be slightly or indeed very different from what the MNE faces at home. This means that it must adapt its output, which has a cost. The standardisation–adaptation decision is central to all international business debate.

Risk diversification

A further strategic driver is the desire to spread risk by working in more than one country at a time. Risk diversification is generally seen as a safe business principle, in part because it helps to avoid over-dependence on a single location or market. For instance and from an upstream, production-side perspective, if a firm has all its industrial assets in one location that suffers a terrible disaster, its situation will be worse than if it also has operations in locations not affected by the disaster. The same applies on the downstream, sales side. A company only selling into one market runs the risk that demand declines there for local reasons, without it having any other customers to pick up the slack. The adversity that a company may experience in one location has less of an effect when it has interests in many others.

Spreading risk through international operations can be done in different ways. Commercially, the Boston Consulting Group has come up with a widely used concept called the "product life cycle", one corollary of which is that a product or service that is expanding in some countries may be declining elsewhere. Clearly, it is advantageous for MNEs to sell into markets where demand is on the rise since they will be able to command higher prices. Otherwise, foreign sales (or production) can offset the foreign exchange risk of accumulating revenues (or liabilities) in the currency of just one country. In short, despite the extra costs and challenges of operating in a foreign environment, diversification means that international business is often a way of reducing risk.

Acquiring inputs

A final international business driver relates to MNEs' need to acquire the resources (materials and labour but also capital and technology) used in their production process. Sometimes this involves inputs that are unavailable in the company's home market. At other times, the cost of an input might be so much lower overseas that a company would be at a competitive disadvantage if, unlike its rivals, it did not source the factor where it is cheapest. The fact that all complex products involve assembling components and modules also means that companies can derive competitive advantage when they source an input from a foreign location that is particularly good at making the item. The end result is that doing business abroad often directly benefits a company's performance at home – making the traditional demarcation between international and domestic business increasingly irrelevant in today's world.

External drivers

Regulatory frameworks

Cross-border transactions can only occur if politics enable them. Traditionally, one of the first responsibilities of any nation-state is to ensure its population's well-being in the face of foreign threats. The main danger is obviously war – but since foreign economic competition can be jarring to a domestic economy, governments will always give thought as well to what level of international business they find acceptable. Broadly speaking, the general paradigm since the early 1980s has been to welcome cross-border flows and allow foreign actors to operate within domestic markets. The trend towards greater "free trade" (or "liberalisation") has meant there are fewer "barriers to entry" today, making it easier for companies to operate on an international scale. At the same time, it is always crucial to keep an eye out for events that might lead to changes in this framework. – one example being the COVID-19 pandemic that erupted in 2020.

The desire for greater cross-border entente has also led to the creation of a global governance regime that itself facilitates international business. One example is the rise of regional trading arrangements (RTAs) like the European Union (EU). RTAs are groups of neighbouring countries that sign agreements enabling easier access to one another's markets. Similarly, there are today a number of trade-friendly international institutions like the World Trade Organisation (WTO), whose laws create a framework in which countries are positively discouraged from adopting isolationist policies. The idea is to construct a system in which cross-border transactions are no longer considered unusual – what the Japanese globalisation theorist Kenichi Ohmae first conceptualised as a "borderless" world. The hope is that this will be a "win–win" for all participating nations. The question then becomes whether this aspiration is always fulfilled.

As aforementioned, there has always been some political resistance to the idea of national borders being opened up to foreign interests that some domestic constituencies may view as rivals. When conflated with the current debate about the value of immigration, this has sparked recent political movements advocating a return to protectionist policies limiting the freedom of foreign companies (and individuals) to cross borders. The future of international business largely depends on whether the current regime based on trade-friendly global institutions remains intact.

Technology

Technology is an umbrella term referring to companies' innovation efforts as well as the technological advances that society as a whole achieves. On MNEs' upstream side, for instance, improved telecommunications have made it possible to stretch value chains to distant locations chosen for their competitive advantage. The same applies to downstream activities, for instance, when the Internet helps to extend a company's customer relationships across borders. Add to this the positive impact that improved logistics have had on trade and it can be argued that technology is one of the main drivers behind the ascendance of international business. This is especially true given how consumers' outlooks and desires often change when they use communications technology and discover how things are done elsewhere. Cross-border comparison has always been a major factor in international business.

Global competition

In the past, when national economies were characterised by greater barriers to trade than they are today, companies would often position themselves vis-à-vis their domestic rivals, competing for a share of the home market. Today, with increasingly penetrable national borders, competitors might come from anywhere. This means that some companies which have worked very hard to raise their productivity or quality levels – and who might still be very competitive in a domestic setting – can suddenly lose market share to hyper-efficient foreign rivals. At the same time, more companies today are enjoying greater opportunities because they too can try to enter their rivals' home markets. In journalist Thomas Friedman's words, today "the world is flat". Everyone's playing field has got bigger.

International finance

Corporate finance has also been affected by these trends. To source the capital needed to run vast multinational empires, MNEs must rely on various funding sources, many of which operate offshore, thus outside of domestic government jurisdiction. The finance industry's deregulation since the 1980 has led to an explosion in cross-border capital flows, much of which is not directly associated with the production of actual goods and services. The partial separation of finance from real business activity has added to the pressures facing MNE managers today.

On one hand, financial asset prices are becoming increasingly volatile hence difficult to predict, adding to the uncertainty of international business. On the other, whereas many MNEs used to be owned by "passive shareholders" mainly interested in safeguarding their investments, today's "shareholder value" paradigm pressures managers into maximising short-term financial returns by running tighter operations and/or taking greater risks. In this way, changes in companies' financial imperatives directly affect the business decisions they make.

Bibliography

Buckley, P. and Casson, M. (2016), *The Future of the Multinational Enterprise*, Basingstoke: Palgrave Macmillan.

Clarke, I. (2014), *The Spatial Organisation of Multinational Corporations*, Abingdon: Routledge.

Fortune magazine (updated annually), Global 500, available at https://fortune.com/global500/

Sitkin, A. and Bowen, N. (2013), *International Business: Challenges and Choices*, Oxford: Oxford University Press.

World Trade Organisation (updated annually), *World Trade Statistical Review*, available at https://www.wto.org/english/res_e/statis_e/wts_e.htm

"That's the way I like it".

2 International business theories

Essential summary

Classical trade theories debate the kinds of economic activities in which different national economies should specialise and the extent to which this should be determined by government or market forces. In more recent times, however, theories have tended to focus on the way in which the location of a given economic activity reflects corporate interests. The background against which different theories are formulated should therefore always be kept in mind, if only because analysts' understanding of the world often depends on the material circumstances they observe at a given point in time. Putting opinions into context has always been a critical skill in international business.

Country-focused trade theories

Thinkers have long grappled with the topic of trade, with some old debates still resonating today. Many ancient Greeks took a dim view of foreign merchants, a reaction known today as xenophobia (from the Greek for fear, *phobia*, and foreign, *xenos*). The philosophers Plato and Xenephon acknowledged the usefulness of establishing an economic division of labour but applied this to individuals, not countries. Aristotle accepted the need for imports but thought they should be limited to certain goods – a forerunner to modern-day interventionism. In general, resistance to foreign trade and/or traders was the norm.

Despite the existence of well-trodden trade routes like the Silk Road running between East and West Asia, general suspicion of merchants would continue for many centuries. Then in Europe, trade's image as a fundamentally immoral activity slowly began to change under the influence of thinkers such as Thomas Aquinas. By the 16th century, legal experts like Spain's Francisco de Vitoria were writing that it is nations' "natural right" to trade with foreigners as long as this did not harm domestic interests. Once this view was legitimised, the door was opened to mercantilism, the first full-fledged trade theory.

Mercantilism

This school of thought dominated from the mid-16th century until sometime around 1776. Its main premise was that the purpose of a national trade policy should be to ensure higher exports than imports, based on the idea that national wealth does not derive from the economic activities that a country hosts but instead from an accumulation of currency (mainly gold at the time) – most of which can only be sourced via trade. In this view, trade is a win–lose proposition. The implication is that a government should use any means possible to better the national trade balance.

The goal of achieving a trade surplus may seem rational yet mercantilism has met with great opposition over the years. The main critique is that it advocates market-distorting state interventions that support uncompetitive vested domestic interests and are also detrimental to consumers. Thomas Mun (1571–1641), a leading mercantilist, was aware of the problems created by governments' standard "defensive" solution of taxing imports to make them more expensive than domestically produced goods. His proposal was that countries should concentrate instead on producing better quality exports. This moved the trade debate to a greater focus on economic efficiency.

A second critique of mercantilism is that history shows countries can prosper even when running a trade deficit. Some analysts at think tanks like the Adam Smith Institute or the Heritage Foundation even believe that a country's trade balance no longer matters and that a more important goal is ensuring corporate profitability. To this day, how trade's benefits are distributed between business interests and society as a whole remains a contentious issue.

Adam Smith's absolute advantage

The founder of "classical" economics is Adam Smith (1723–1790), a Scotsman whose seminal work from 1776, *The Wealth of Nations*, set the table for many economic and trade principles that are still being used today. A keen observer of Britain's changes during the first Industrial

Revolution, Smith strongly opposed mercantilism, which he accused of falsifying competition and rewarding inefficient "vested interests". Smith believed that governments should stay out of markets, which he saw as being driven by individuals' pursuit of self-interest (called their "utility"). In his view, the "hand of God" helps markets to naturally tend towards an optimal allocation of resources (called "equilibrium"). In this scenario, the best way to enhance overall efficiency is to allow uncompetitive industries to die naturally and invest instead in sectors with good growth prospects (a process that Austrian economist Joseph Schumpeter later referred to as "creative destruction").

The strength of Smith's theory is his idea that efficiency goes hand-in-hand with specialisation achieved through a "division of labour". This applies to both domestic economics and international trade. The famous example Smith used to demonstrate the latter involved two countries that each have an "absolute advantage" in producing different goods (the British textiles, the Portuguese wine). In this view, it would be in both countries' interest to import one another's speciality product instead of making it at home. Smith's proposition is substantiated every time a country uses a cheap imported component in its domestic production process instead of manufacturing the same component locally but at a higher cost. The foreign component actually strengthens the local economy.

Despite its strengths, Smith's absolute advantage theory remains imperfect. In the real world, advantages are distributed unevenly, with some countries enjoying greater factor endowments (like land, capital or natural resources) than others. This inequality is sometimes size-related, with larger countries often having greater access to factors like labour (China) or natural resources (Russia and Australia). Whatever the cause, there is no question that some countries are relatively handicapped in the face of international competition, raising the question of why they would even want to open their borders to foreign rivals. Moreover, analysing nations in terms of natural advantage is a static view. Countries and/or entrepreneurs are capable of acquiring new advantages (especially technology). Japan, for example, has few natural resources yet is an economic powerhouse. This is something that would be hard to predict using Smith's absolute advantage principles.

A second problem with Smith's theory involves the social and political consequences of countries abandoning entire swathes of economic activity to foreign producers – an issue that became particularly topical when the COVID-19 pandemic created problems for countries unable to produce certain strategic goods (like medical supplies) domestically. Smith was very probably correct that specialisation improves efficiency – but that is, of course, of little consolation to workers losing their jobs in the sectors that their country abandons. As the political economist J. M. Keynes wrote, the problem with long-term equilibrium is that "in the long run we are all dead." Classical theorists like Smith may feel that markets have their own laws, but it is difficult to argue that they can exist independently of political and social realities.

A final weakness in Smith's construct is the fact that countries lacking absolute advantage – or suffering from poor terms of trade due to their specialisation in low-value-added sectors – will be too poor to buy the goods that their more competitive counterparts produce. To organise a successful market, it is not enough to have efficient producers, as Smith thought. There must also be solvent customers with money to spend.

Comparative advantage

David Ricardo's *Principles of Political Economy and Taxation* (1817) created the idea of "comparative advantage" that remains the basis of many modern trade models. The great novelty of Ricardo's work was its vision of international trading as a win–win proposition that under certain conditions benefits all countries, even less competitive ones. In this view, the absence of absolute advantage no longer precludes participation in international trade since a country can still occupy a sector as long as domestic workers' wages are adjusted to reflect their lesser efficiency. This was a first step towards resolving the problems associated with Smith's absolute advantage construct.

Like Smith, Ricardo used a wine versus textiles example to prove his theory (see Figure 2.1). Unlike Smith, he started with the premise that Portugal produces both goods more cheaply than England. Ricardo then asked why England should open its borders if it has no absolute advantage in either market. The answer was that in addition to the

	Wine costs	Textiles cost	Domestic price structure	At international price of 1 wine unit = 0.75 textile unit
In Portugal	5	10	1 wine unit = 0.5 textile units (5/10)	Receives extra 0.25 textile units when export 1 wine unit
In England	15	15	1 wine unit = 1 textile unit (15/15)	Receives extra 1.33 wine units (1/0.75) when exporting 1 textile unit

Figure 2.1 A basic Ricardian model.

necessity of finding comparatively inefficient countries something to export (so they can make money enabling them to purchase efficient countries' exports), there is a certain price at which the opportunity cost of this approach is minimised and everyone benefits.

This too is a strong but imperfect theory, criticised because it ignores factors such as capital mobility and technological transfers. These are important insofar as they affect the international distribution of comparative advantage. It remains that there are many real-life examples of Ricardo's theory at work today. One is the Russian agricultural sector, which produces both cereals and farm equipment less competitively than its French counterpart. Under Smith's theorem, Russia would have to import both goods from France. In actual fact, it imports tractors but exports grains since its productivity disadvantage in grains costs less than its disadvantage in tractors. It is a real-life outcome perfectly predictable under Ricardo's theorem.

Infant industries

The English philosopher John Stuart Mill's main contribution to international trade theory was the infant industry argument he formulated at the same time as German economist Friedrich List. In Mill's opinion, the one time government intervention is justified comes when a country needs to protect industries that are brand new hence vulnerable to foreign competition. As he wrote in 1848 in *The Principles of Political Economy*,

> The superiority of one country over another in a branch of production often arises only from having begun sooner. There may be no inherent advantage on one part, or disadvantage on the other, but only a present superiority of acquired skill and experience.

This idea is relevant to modern concerns about the ability of a country – most poignantly, an emerging Global South nation – to enter sectors where others already have a head start. Examples include South Korea, which over the second half of the 20th century evolved from a poor agricultural economy to become a global technological powerhouse.

Trade and social welfare

Underlying Smith's theory is the optimistic idea that a properly functioning market economy benefits society as a whole. Conversely, Ricardo's observation that some social classes are more dynamic than others recognises the possibility of an uneven distribution of economic benefits. German philosopher Karl Marx (1818–1883) expanded upon this latter point, stating that the starting point for all analysis should be capitalism's exploitation of one social segment by another. Marx's pessimistic worldview probably explains his absence from many international business textbooks. Yet his words still resonate today when nations are accused of using open border globalisation as a smoke screen for domination. It would be a mistake to study market capitalism without considering its leading critic.

One Marxian theory with direct relevance to international business today is the "law of diminishing returns", which holds that a firm operating in a closed capitalist economy necessarily suffers from declining profit rates. In this view, firms must internationalise to survive. The theorem is largely disproved, however, by Joseph Schumpeter's 1912 demonstration of how "technological progress" can sustain growth within a national framework – a key factor in certain explanations of MNE location decisions.

A 20th century variant of Marx's doubts about the benefits of global free markets can be seen in the writings of the Brazilian Raul Prebisch, who argued that free trade is bad because it creates "dependency" relationships. Partially in response to this, a more recent school of thought called "welfare economics" has sought compromise by offering a less political and more economic debate about free markets' degree of fairness. Expanding upon notions of "optimality" developed in 1895 by the Italian economist, Vilfredo Pareto, this new school is led by US Nobel laureates Joseph Stiglitz, who analysed the "discontents of globalisation", and Paul Krugman, who argues that those who benefit from open borders should compensate those who suffer from them. An ancillary theorem has been developed by Indian philosopher Amartya Sen, whose Human Development Index contends that standards of living cannot be assessed using purely numerical indicators like GDP – what matters instead are the benefits accruing to the whole of society. Interestingly, economists Jagdish Bhagwati and Hernando de Soto support this aspiration even as they assert that it can best be achieved by expanding market systems characterised by enforceable contracts. The common feature of all these outlooks, with their varying assessment of the fairness of free trade, is that theories of economic efficiency are inoperative unless they maximise social utility.

Factor proportions (Heckscher–Ohlin)

Swedish economists Eli Heckscher (1879–1952) and Bertil Ohlin (1899–1979) devised a model stating that, when two countries trade, each will export the good that makes the most intensive use of the particular factor input (labour, capital or natural resources) that it possesses in abundance. This is because each can source the abundant factor cheaply, thereby becoming more competitive in sectors where that factor is key. Conversely, a country should import the good that makes the most intensive use of the factor input which is most scarce locally.

An example of the Hekscher–Ohlin (H–O) model might be that France, where capital is abundant, tends to specialise in factory-made carpets, whereas Turkey, where labour is abundant (hence wages low), tends to produce handmade rugs. At its simplest level, this elegant model is central to modern neo-classical trade theory. Unfortunately and as the Russian economist Wassily Leontieff pointed out, it is not always capable of explaining real-life behaviour. H–O only seems to really work when cross-border differences in productivity and technology are introduced – elements that depend in part on business behaviour.

Modern business-centred theories

The leading international business theories over the past half-century have focused more on corporate behaviour than on national economies. This may reflect the rising wealth of MNEs and declining power of national governments.

Product life cycle

In a persuasive article published in 1966, Raymond Vernon linked international manufacturing location decisions to a "product life cycle" (PLC). The theory asserts that production location decisions have less to do with national specialisation and more with how a company feels about a product's relative innovativeness, the resulting need for confidentiality, the margins that can be commanded and the priority accorded to cost control (see Figure 2.2). Note that these are all determinations made by MNE managers – a change from earlier theories that tended to ignore corporate deliberations.

Stage	1. Introduction	2. Growth	3. Maturity	4. Decline
Market dynamics	High-priced new good	Demand spreads	Competition intensifies	Demand declines
Key to success	R&D, confidentiality	Market coverage	Rejuvenation via marketing	Low prices
Production location(s)	Global North home country	Throughout Global North	Both Global North and South	Global South only

Figure 2.2 The four stages in Vernon's product life cycle theory.

Vernon's theory is interesting but does not apply in all circumstances. Products with a short life span (like microprocessors) may not survive long enough to experience the entire PLC. Also, products like luxury goods, whose perceived value is highly influenced by marketing, may not age in the way the model predicts. The idea that a product can, at a given point in time, simultaneously find itself at different stages of its life cycle in different countries is a valuable one, however.

New trade theory

The starting point for much New Trade Theory is John Dunning's 1977 proposal of an "Eclectic Paradigm", itself partially derived from earlier analysis by Stephen Hymer regarding the advantages for firms of maintaining control over their internal capabilities. The idea here is that because markets often function imperfectly, MNEs are likelier to face higher costs in foreign markets than domestic firms do. In this case, FDI is only attractive if internationalisation offers specific incentives:

Ownership advantages: The MNE must have a special product or manufacturing process that it can use against home market rivals. This explains why technologically advanced companies guard their secrets so jealously.

Location advantages: Moving production abroad must offer advantages like greater economies of scale.

Internalisation advantages: It must be useful for the MNE to exploit the ownership advantage itself instead of licensing or selling it to someone else. The company must want to control a larger portion of its overall value chain.

In Dunning's wake, James Markusen's "gravity model" observed that most trade and FDI occurs between neighbouring countries featuring similar levels of socioeconomic development. This contradicts classical economists' predictions that trade is likely to occur between countries that are very different in nature. Markusen found that, as often than not, FDI involves "horizontal integration", where companies make similar goods at home and abroad, rather than "vertical integration" where different international units intervene at different value chain stages. He concluded that the key factor in MNE internationalisation is "knowledge capital" – a finding substantiated by the disproportionate concentration of MNEs in research-oriented high-tech sectors like computing or pharmaceuticals where intangible, firm-specific assets are key. This is because knowledge can be transferred more easily and inexpensively than other forms of capital, with such transfers also being an effective way of giving MNEs "first-mover advantage" in the new markets they enter.

Unlike Heckscher–Ohlin's emphasis on national factor endowments, the New Trade Theory's main explanation for a company's international success is its ability to apply knowledge worldwide. This introduces the notion that the location of a particular activity may be a consequence of corporate decision-making and have less to do with absolute or comparative advantage. The emphasis here is on the human element – opening the door to "behavioural" analysis injecting human psychology and other social sciences into international business analysis – a multi-disciplinary approach that the present book very much supports.

Competitive advantage

Michael Porter's 1990 study, *The Competitive Advantage of Nations*, focuses less on FDI than on the connection between countries' relative endowments in capital, natural resources and labour, on one hand, and MNEs' historical development, on the other. Porter's "Diamond" identifies four sources of competitive advantage, some relating to external factors and others reflecting corporate actions:

Factor endowments. Porter distinguished between basic inputs (natural resources, climate) and advanced, productivity-enhancing inputs translating countries' long-term investments in technology and education. In his opinion, this latter category, largely developed in response to pressures that countries face to make better use of their natural factor endowments, is the main driver of national competitive advantage.

Demand conditions. Variables here are a domestic market's size and buyers' sophistication. MNE starting from large home markets characterised by demanding consumers are better equipped to succeed abroad.

Related and supporting industry. This was probably Porter's most useful insight. Firms benefit from the proximity of "clusters" of efficient upstream suppliers offering inexpensive components and "knowledge spillovers".

Firm strategy, structure and rivalry. A firm's managerial orientation (focus on finance, engineering, etc.) is crucial to its success. Also, companies that hone their skills against tough domestic rivals compete better abroad.

Porter's theory is rational but does not explain why failures still occur even when the conditions he outlines have been fulfilled. Clearly there are other factors at work as well – one strong possibility being the "organisational learning" that Chapter 7 explores in further detail.

Bibliography

Baldwin, R. and Domeji, D. (2008), *The Development and Testing of Heckscher–Ohlin Trade Models*, Cambridge, MA: MIT Press.

Kemp, M. (2008), *International Trade Theory: A Critical Review*, London: Routledge.

Mill, J.S. (1848), *Principles of Political Economy*, London: John William Parker (publisher).

Ricardo, D. (1817), *The Principles of Political Economy and Taxation*, London: John Murray (publisher).

Smith, A. (1776), *The Wealth of Nations*, London: William Strahan and Thomas Cadell (publishers).

"Remind me, which one are we selling to?"
"Probably the same as the one we're buying from".

3 The politics of international business

Essential summary

Companies operate in frameworks defined by national and international laws, regulations and institutions created to address a wide range of policy objectives and reflecting different political ideologies. As discussed in Chapter 2, the big debate in international business has long been to what extent nation-states seek to protect domestic producers from foreign competition or, conversely, want to open their borders to trade and FDI. In turn, this often reflects different attitudes towards the legitimacy of state intervention in the economy – a construct that the World Bank tries to quantify through its "Ease of Doing Business" index. This chapter begins with a review of the paradigms guiding international business-related policy-making before looking at the various interventionist tools that nation-states can wield if they so desire. It concludes with a study of the global governance regimes established to address the supranational aspects of international business politics.

What economic role for government

Debates over government's ideal economic role are crucial to understanding the political framework within which international business operates. Broadly speaking, the two main schools of thought in this area hold either that government should let market actors run most if not all economic decision-making (a philosophy often referred to as "laissez-faire" or "neo-liberalism") or else that it has a duty to weigh in on economic activities in order to achieve certain policy outcomes (a philosophy that might be called "interventionism"). It is crucial to note that this debate plays out at both a national and an international level, and that it is possible for a government to pursue one philosophy at home and another abroad – a hybrid approach exemplified by the kind of "developmental capitalism" that has marked the recent political history of certain emerging economies like Malaysia or Thailand, where international openness has been combined with domestic interventionism. Similarly, it is important to remember that domestic policies implemented within a national territory remain relevant to international business, if only because they affect how MNEs might operate in that one country as opposed to others.

Cycles in economic thinking

Attitudes towards the legitimacy of state intervention vary in time and place (see Figure 3.1). In the early 20th century, for instance, many politicians in the world's leading power of the day, the UK, believed in minimal government action. This applied not only to trade but also to the domestic economy, viewed by classical economists as a natural phenomenon best left untouched.

Such passivity came under widespread criticism when the 1929 Wall Street Crash was followed by the Great Depression. The crisis led to calls for new economic policy, one where the capitalist state would be empowered to manage the business cycle proactively. The end result was a resurgence of interventionism, largely driven by the ideas of British economist John Maynard Keynes, who believed that government's first priority is to address those short-term human needs that markets do not satisfy, in part by using deficit spending to maintain aggregate

Laissez-faire	Crisis = Shift	Interventionism	Crisis = Shift	Laissez-faire	Crisis = Shift?
Classical economics, Globalisation's first wave	Depression, WWII	Keynesianism, post-War boom	Oil shocks, stagflation	Neoliberalism, Globalisation's second wave	Credit crunch, state debt; COVID-19 pandemic
c. 1880-1929	1929-1945	1945-1970s	1970s	1970s-2008	2008-?

Figure 3.1 Dominant economic policy paradigms have evolved in response to crises.

demand during recessions, with the ensuing debt to be repaid via higher taxes cooling the economy down during upswings.

By the mid-20th century, Keynesianism had become the dominant paradigm in much of the capitalist world. The new consensus was that states could and should control many domestic sectors; develop welfare systems; engage in economic planning; and even manage entire industrial sectors. State involvement often went far beyond Keynes's original advice but criticisms remained muted as long as economies boomed – as many did for 30 years following World War II.

Once again, it was an economic crisis that changed dominant thinking about the state's ideal role. The global economy slumped in the 1970s, beleaguered by high oil prices, budget deficits, inflation, unemployment and saturated markets. This led to widespread disenchantment with Keynesianism and renewed support for classical economics, renamed neo-liberalism. The end result was the election in 1979 and 1980 of UK Prime Minister Margaret Thatcher and US President Ronald Reagan, influenced by economists such as Friedrich Hayek and the monetarist, Milton Friedman, who thought that a state's main priority was to ensure stable prices and not promote welfare directly. Laissez-faire ideology was back in fashion in domestic politics but also internationally, with the decades following 1980 marked by most countries worldwide reducing trade barriers, often mediated by the offices of an intergovernmental organisation. In particular, many Global South nations that had previously been run according to protectionist principles designed to protect these newly independent countries from (neo-)colonial domination switched to more trade-friendly policies that helped to accelerate their economic development at a record pace, taking billions of people worldwide out of abject poverty. By the late 20th century, there seemed to be a global political consensus regarding the benefits of international business.

The question today is how long trade and FDI-friendly politics will dominate. History teaches that paradigms last for only as long as enough people believe in them. The global financial crisis that erupted in 2008 as a result of poor bank supervision led to governments worldwide running up huge debt to shore up their financial systems and avoid a 1929-style depression. The reduction in public spending that followed as governments sought to contain this debt weakened the social safety networks protecting many Global North countries' less affluent populations. Note that these constituencies' job and wage prospects were already being undermined because – in the view of Nobel laureate Joseph Stiglitz – generations of laissez-faire politicians had rejected the kinds of redistributive policies that could have seen globalisation's beneficiaries compensate, in the name of social cohesion, their fellow citizens suffering from the combined effects of automation and foreign competition. The ensuing disenchantment facilitated the rise of protectionist interventionism in the mid-2010s, with new political figures (most notably Donald Trump in the United States and Brexit advocates in the UK) convincing some voters that globalisation was the main if not single culprit for their problems. The same narrative could also be heard in early 2020 in the attribution of blame for the COVID-19 pandemic. Robust evidence exists demonstrating that these explanations are simplistic to the point of being false. The big question for the years to come then becomes how long this misrepresentation of economic reality might continue to dominate political discourse.

The future of international business politics

The question is especially poignant given the objective drivers that, notwithstanding certain demagogic political discourses, may well encourage further growth in international business volumes. One such factor is information technology, which empowers manufacturers and consumers to shop across national borders, often causing them to purchase cheaper better quality items abroad, despite certain politicians' efforts to orient demand towards domestic producers. Another is the growing deregulation of the financial markets, with companies freer than ever to transfer capital across borders, thereby escaping political authorities whose jurisdiction is largely restricted to their national territories.

This latter point is crucial to the future politics of international business. MNEs generally have an advantage over national governments since they are not tied to any particular location and have a choice of where they might invest. Through the practice of "regime shopping", MNEs can play countries off against one another to get the best deal for themselves. A frequent criticism of this asymmetrical relationship is that it creates a "race to the bottom", with cash-strapped governments being successfully lobbied by powerful MNEs to weaken social and environmental standards and lower tax rates. Of course, this power relationship is reversed when the country is characterised by a large, dynamic market and the MNE is not offering anything unique.

It is worth noting that after rising constantly for more or less 40 years, the percentage of total global economic activity accounted for by international business started flatlining around 2015, possibly indicating that this trend has reached its limits. Domestic business remains vital in today's world, especially in service sectors which may be harder to internationalise than manufacturing activities. Notwithstanding MNEs' decades-long move towards cross-border economic integration, the world remains far from borderless, with national governments continuing to perform key governmental roles (like regulation and taxation) shaping MNEs' business environments. On top of this, numerous studies point to many consumers' ongoing loyalty to more familiar domestic brands. The most accurate way of depicting the current politics of international business is therefore to highlight the tension that exists between the undeniable benefits of cross-border economic integration and the continued attraction of what French politician Bernard Carayon famously termed "economic patriotism". An interesting part of this debate is the possibility that a subjective emotion like national pride can be as important to economic decision-making as rational value-for-money calculations.

In most countries nowadays, governments tend to resolve this tension somewhere in the middle. Few regimes advocate self-sufficient "autarky" rejecting all international business. At the same time, even the most trade and FDI-friendly governments understand their responsibility to protect national self-interest (like domestic employment) using whole array of tools designed towards this end. Given how often international business politics focuses on countries' deployment of such tools, their analysis is useful to learners in this field.

International business intervention tools

Some tools, like import quotas and anti-dumping provisions, specifically target trade. Others, like ownership restrictions, only apply to FDI. Lastly, some intervention tools, like subsidies and macro-economic policies, are more general and affect the economy as a whole.

Trade tools

The main difference at this level is whether a foreign actor must pay a sum of money or is being subjected to administrative controls.

Tariffs

Tariffs (or customs duties) are usually assessed on an "ad valorem" basis as a percentage of a shipment's value. They can also be "specific" and represent a lump sum for a given physical quantity. National governments often use tariffs to try to modify international trade patterns and orient their domestic economies towards more lucrative activities that improve the country's terms of trade by increasing the value-added generated by the particular activities in which it specialises. This orientation has countless examples in history, one notable example being the protectionist arguments formulated by the politician Alexander Hamilton at the birth of the American republic. Note that to avoid penalising domestic industries that import basic inputs (e.g. leather), tariffs tend to be higher on goods that have reached a more advanced stage of processing (e.g. shoes).

By artificially making foreign goods more expensive, tariffs affect domestic consumers' product preferences. This makes them a key topic in international negotiations, with notable recent examples being the increased price of imported Chinese solar panels or European steel in the United States once Donald Trump began implementing his policy of aggressive trade wars.

Non-tariff barriers (NTBs)

Quantitative restrictions: The two main variants are Voluntary Export Restraints (VERs) and import quotas. VERs refer to one country's agreement to limit the volume and/or value of its exports to another country, usually to avoid the kind of hostile response that trade imbalances provoke. Import quotas specify the maximum quantity of a good that a country is prepared to import.

By restricting the supply of a foreign good, VERs and import quotas increase its price to domestic consumers. This means extra revenue for foreign sellers. On the other hand, when import tariffs are applied, it is the domestic government that pockets the surcharge, in the form of taxes collected as the good enters the country. In this sense, tariffs are a more effective way of protecting national interests than quotas.

Standards: Where consumer health is at stake, governments often require scientific evidence that a product is safe. Problems arise when one country accuses another of misusing such controls to disguise protectionist intentions – exemplified by American assessment of the EU's environmentalist policy of refusing to import chlorinated chicken

Anti-dumping provisions: Companies sometimes try to gain market share by dumping goods at artificially low prices. The problem is determining whether an import is cheap because foreign producers are manipulating prices or simply because they are able to manufacture the product less expensively. The issue has become particularly poignant in a world where Global South countries characterised by low labour costs have increased their share of Global North markets.

Lastly, a number of NTBs are more administrative in nature. These include product labelling, rules of origin requirements and assorted bureaucratic controls.

FDI tools

Some interventionist tools put controls on MNE subsidiaries. This has become necessary due to FDI's growing role in world economic activity.

Performance requirements

Local contents ratios. MNEs must ensure that a minimum percentage of the value of the goods they sell in the host country comes from locally sourced components.

Dividend repatriation regulations. Restrictions on the quantity of money that an MNE can take out of a country in the form of dividends.

Technology transfers. Here the goal is to ensure that MNEs bring knowledge into the host country and/or undertake research locally.

Employment measures. Initiatives aimed at accelerating recruitment, improving pay scales or enhancing worker training.

Ownership restrictions

These tools range from limiting MNEs' stake in local ventures to the expropriation of foreign companies' local units. In many countries, the FDI environment is influenced by competition regulators who seek to ensure that foreign interests do not abuse their power. Policies of this sort are usually justified by a desire to protect domestic competition. Often enough, however, their real purpose is to protect domestic competitors.

Macro-economic policy

A country's trading position is affected by its government's general economic policies. Tax systems, for example, can be used to shift domestic demand towards home-made products (e.g. by raising VAT on the items that the country traditionally imports). Special "free trade zones" can be set up, allowing companies to import components destined for re-exportation on a tax-free basis. Countries might keep their currency artificially low to facilitate exports or raise it to lower import costs. Many national economic decisions are taken with a view towards achieving international outcomes – and vice versa.

Governments also have a number of targeted competitiveness schemes at their disposal. Examples include workforce training programmes; payroll tax relief for exporters; preferential treatment for domestic companies bidding on public procurement contracts; and export assistance packages targeting local small and medium-sized enterprises (SMEs). Governments might also try to alter domestic consumer behaviour through "buy local" campaigns.

Subsidies

The most common variety of trade-related government subsidies involves direct payments to domestic exporters and/or producers operating in sectors that suffer from foreign competition. This can be contentious, however, if subsidies enabling uncompetitive companies to stay alive are considered market-distorting. In situations where producers in one country lose market share to a subsidised foreign rival, their government might try to offset this advantage by fining the company in question. Penalties of this kind, called "countervailing duties", are supposed to restore fairness. The complication is that in certain situations, for instance, where infant industries are involved, it is actually the subsidies that re-establish a level playing field.

What becomes clear in the assessment of these tools' implementation is that actions which one country may deem necessary to ensure the fairness of an international transaction might be considered, quite understandably, as unfair by its trading partners. A basic principle in all economic transactions, and above all in international business, is reciprocity, or the idea that the only way to ensure a deal's viability is for all parties to benefit from it. Nation-states are not in the business of handing out favours without getting something in return – with history having taught most policymakers that a good way to achieve this kind of reciprocity is by establishing intergovernmental organisations (IGOs) and regional associations (RAs) mandated to devise international business policies on a supranational level.

Global governance

Rather than equating the rise of IGOs and RAs with a decline in individual nation-states' political power, there is a strong argument that the shift to a multilateral system improves many governments' bargaining power. This applies both to smaller countries whose voice is strengthened by membership in IGOs and to poorer Global South nations negotiating with powerful MNEs and/or Global North countries.

Intergovernmental organisations

International business policy-making is influenced by IGOs as varied as the United Nations and the World Health Organisation, but the organisations that arguably have the greatest impact are the ones that came out of the 1947 Bretton Woods conference, namely the World Bank, the International Monetary Fund and above all the World Trade Organisation (WTO). Whereas the first two specialise in providing borrowers with funding (respectively long-term development capital and short-term crisis finance), the WTO – which grew out of the General Agreement and Trade and Tariffs to become a full-fledged bureaucracy in 1996 – defines its functions as administering trade agreements, hosting negotiations, arbitrating disputes, monitoring national policies and offering technical assistance. Its main goal is to maximise international business and prevent member-states from adopting discriminatory trade policies. This is easier said than done, however, given differences of opinion regarding which sectors of economic activity should be liberalised as a priority. Current bones of contention include the WTO tolerating Global North nations' ongoing protection of their domestic agricultural sectors even as they try to force their Global South counterparts to open up the latter's service sectors. The end result is that the WTO's ability to further expand its free trade agenda has more or less ground to a halt. Having said that, its Dispute Resolution Mechanism has been very effective at arbitrating most international trade disputes – at least until recently, when this trade tribunal came under attack from politicians such as Donald Trump disputing the WTO's basic premise that international cooperation produces better outcomes than nationalism.

Regional associations

RAs' policy scope varies widely, ranging from a accords where participants simply agree to reduce barriers to trade on one or just a few items, to comprehensive arrangements rivalling and sometimes superseding national governments' own policy-making remits (see Figure 3.2).

The world's most integrated RA is the European Union (EU), legitimised in part by the premise that regional loyalty is possible above and beyond national sovereignty. The EU's remit is therefore wider than a purely economic RA's would be and many of its subsidiaries are endowed with supranational political powers. Having said that, the EU's main achievements have been in the field of international business, whether this involves the increased competitiveness of European companies able to construct efficient and competitive supply chains based on seamless intra-European trade, or else the EU's strong representation of member-states' interests in trade and FDI negotiations with third parties. As shown by Brexit, voices do exist that criticise the EU for taking a modicum of political sovereignty away from national governments. This opinion is rejected, however, by most international business practitioners and indeed by the quasi-totality of Nobel Prize economists, aghast at the idea that in this day and age a country like the

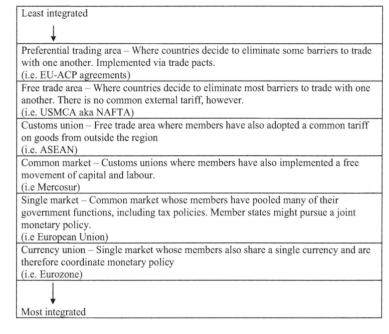

Least integrated ↓
Preferential trading area – Where countries decide to eliminate some barriers to trade with one another. Implemented via trade pacts. (i.e. EU-ACP agreements)
Free trade area – Where countries decide to eliminate most barriers to trade with one another. There is no common external tariff, however. (i.e. USMCA aka NAFTA)
Customs union – Free trade area where members have also adopted a common tariff on goods from outside the region (i.e. ASEAN)
Common market – Customs unions where members have also implemented a free movement of capital and labour. (i.e Mercosur)
Single market – Common market whose members have pooled many of their government functions, including tax policies. Member states might pursue a joint monetary policy. (i.e European Union)
Currency union – Single market whose members also share a single currency and are therefore coordinate monetary policy (i.e. Eurozone)
↓ Most integrated

Figure 3.2 Regional agreements with varying degrees of integration.

UK is willingly erecting barriers to trade with its closest neighbours. It is an anomaly again demonstrating the blurring of economics and politics in international business.

Bibliography

European Union website home page, https://europa.eu/

Hayek, F. (1944), *The Road to Serfdom*, Chicago: University of Chicago Press

Heydon, K. and Woolcock, S. (2017), *The Ashgate Research Companion to International Trade Policy*, Abingdon: Routledge.

Keynes, J. M. (1936), *The General Theory of Employment, Interest and Money*, London: Palgrave Macmillan.

World Trade Organisation website home page, https://www.wto.org/

"You sure it's the same company?"

4 Ethics and international business

Essential summary

In international business, ethics – the set of moral principles governing behaviour and decision-making processes – relates to the definition and transfer of value systems across borders. For people to interact harmoniously (including in a business context), they must have certain values in common and learn to manage whatever differences remain. More problematic is determining which values should govern cross-border dealings in a world featuring such diverse economic, political, social and legal cultures. Relativism is a serious complication in all of international business – particularly where perceptions of ethical conduct are concerned.

International business ethics are challenging on several levels. One is the question whether the benefits that an MNE generates through its activities – creating jobs and products, paying wages and taxes, etc. – compensate for the damage that some of its practices or outcomes may cause. This is especially hard to determine given that actions considered appropriate in some societies may be deemed unsuitable in others – a variability making it difficult for companies to devise codes of conduct that will be relevant under all circumstances. There is also the question of whether firms should be free to define their own Corporate Social Responsibility (CSR) agenda or if this should be imposed on them – and if so, by whom.

The debate over (international) business ethics

"Ethical confusion" arises when employees are unclear about – and/or do not agree with – what their employer expects of them. People often join a firm specifically because they identify with its values but at some point, they might be pressured into decisions at odds with their personal ethics. The same problem happens in international business when corporate (or personal) ethics are at odds with the values that dominate within a particular national culture. Hence the need to analyse international business ethics not only at the personal, national and corporate levels but also with respect to how these planes interact – if only to develop analysis of whether certain ethical expectations might be deemed absolute or, instead, need to be relativised.

Ethics vary in time and place

Business ethics can only be studied in context. Practices like child labour that are widely criticised in Europe today were widespread before 19th century reformers first began denouncing them. As theorised in US economist Simon Kuznets' famous "curve", a country desperate to industrialise might accept higher levels of corruption or pollution than it will when it achieves greater affluence. Much behaviour is only considered unethical once its uglier aspects has been revealed – and/or after the society afflicted by the behaviour has surpassed a certain level of well-being and therefore develops more demanding expectations of corporate behaviour.

A watershed moment for business ethics came in the early 20th century when the rise of large, multi-divisional firms caused owners and managers' roles to separate, with the latter often being considered more ethical because they were assumed to have greater interest in how their actions affected the local community. With the "shareholder value" and "financialisation" paradigms that arose in the 1980s, today there seems to be greater alignment between managers and shareholders' interests. This is partially due to the proliferation in certain countries of profit-sharing bonus schemes that motivate managers to prioritise profitability to the exclusion of broader societal considerations. The first rule of international business ethics is that they can only be understood accurately in light of actors' financial but also non-financial incentives to behave ethically in different situations and locations.

It is also crucial to analyse, in line with the famous Theory of Justice formulated by the philosopher John Rawls, the distribution of cost and benefits associated with certain behaviours. In some cases, for instance, an action can create tremendous advantages for a lucky few but slightly harm many others. Other actions might offer almost everyone a small benefit but greatly damage a few people. How these arbitrages are adjudicated worldwide is a further component of international business ethics.

Lastly, it is worth noting that certain business ethics dilemmas are specifically international in nature. One is when a powerful MNE tries to bully a poor government into lowering taxes and/or regulatory standards, threatening to take much-needed investment elsewhere if the country does not offer advantageous market entry conditions. "Regime shopping" of this kind puts pressure on desperate host governments to abandon one crucial need (clean environment, workers' health and safety) in the hope of satisfying another (foreign capital). Forcing countries into these kinds of trade-offs is often considered ethically dubious.

The case for and against explicit CSR

The growing demand for ethics in business has in recent years markedly increased global support for corporate social responsibility (CSR) actions materialising this sentiment. Yet not everyone agrees. Opponents include laissez-faire thinkers who feel that CSR is wrong because businesses should focus on profitability alone, and cynics who see CSR as a way of diverting people's attention from corporate misconduct. The relative strength of these two outlooks varies in different countries.

Anti-CSR

A few decades ago, one of the authors of this book suggested launching a corporate recycling scheme, only to be criticised for "wasting time" by his boss who argued that employees should think solely about making money. It is fair to say that CSR has not always been a popular topic in certain business circles.

Neo-liberal think tanks, for instance, have in the past accused CSR supporters of not giving firms sufficient credit for the taxes and wages they pay. On top of this, development economists have questioned whether forcing MNEs to engage in CSR spending is the right priority for the world's poorer countries who have yet to achieve a certain level of material well-being. Most famously, CSR was criticised by economist Milton Friedman because he felt that spending in this arena reduced shareholder dividends, slashed workers' pay and increased consumer prices. Friedmann argued instead that all companies need to do is act legally, with government alone being responsible for managing the social and environmental consequences of corporate behaviour.

Pro-CSR

The problem with Friedman's critique is he over-simplified the role played by the rule of law. Laws have never been absolute but simply reflect the consensus zeitgeist in a given society at a given moment in time – an accord that can be distorted if an asymmetrical power relationship exists between government and business. A much more useful measurement for MNEs is therefore "ethical compliance" (see Figure 4.1), which monitors the relationship between an MNE's ethics and/or CSR actions, and the standards it negotiates with a host government.

A further weakness of Friedman's position is that it does not reflect the majority opinion in international business today. Many if not most business people seem to have finally accepted that CSR actions are more of a necessity than a luxury. Whether this is because of their personal ethics or because they want to spare their company criticism is uncertain – and also not necessarily important, unless one is of the opinion that a lack of authenticity will encourage inaccurate, "greenwashing" publicity where the company will depict itself as being more ethical than it really is.

There are many positive reasons for MNEs to engage in CSR. First and foremost is that by so doing they stand to burnish their reputation with all the benefits this generates in terms of brand image, recruitment, staff motivation and stakeholder relationships. Companies know that if they are not liked or trusted by consumers they may well lose business (especially if they have a chequered history from which their

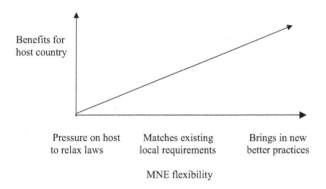

Figure 4.1 "Degree of 'ethical compliance'".

reputation still suffers) – but conversely, if they can be seen as good citizens, they create "amenity value", producing a "halo effect" that is likely to win them goodwill.

Conversely, where MNEs do not behave ethically and/or engage in CSR, nowadays they risk a number of criticisms. First, with MNEs controlling such a large proportion of today's global economy, some voices feel they are duty-bound to attend to the social, environmental and other problems faced by the societies where their actions will be felt. This is especially important today, given the insufficiency of government resources (partly attributable to MNEs paying lower tax rates than in the past) – a phenomenon that the political scientist Susan Strange famously referred to as "the retreat of the state", exacerbated by the COVID-19 pandemic's devastating effects on government budgets. Second, there is the simple fact that MNEs' power means many populations worldwide will be affected by any negative "externalities" they may produce (i.e. pollution). This can easily translate into public disproval of an MNE accused of misconduct – disgruntlement that CSR helps to dissipate. Third, it is difficult to find any moral justification for exempting MNEs shareholders from the same social responsibilities as everyone else bears. After all, there is the risk that in the absence of positive CSR, MNEs might calculate that they need not do their utmost to protect society: either because they want a "free ride" and expect government to compensate victims of their misconduct on their behalf; or because the profits from such actions exceed any penalties.

Ultimately, the possibility for MNEs to behave unethically and get away with it is very low in today's 24/7 news world. Most business schools training tomorrow's international managers understand how important CSR has become, as witnessed by the growth of sustainability studies. In addition and as observed by Cambridge sociologist Noreena Hertz, at the very least MNE employees can generally be expected to bring their personal ethics with themselves into the workplace. In the early 21st century, CSR has clearly gone mainstream – albeit to varying degrees across the world.

International CSR in practice

MNEs' main ethical dilemmas

Human rights

One serious dilemma for MNEs is whether they should refuse to do business with countries that violate the principles of liberty and humanity put forth by the United Nations in its 1948 Declaration of

Human Rights. The challenge here is determining the net effect of MNEs operating in countries where abuses are rampant. On one hand, MNEs refusing to work with such regimes might be starving the local economy of much needed capital, jobs and technology. At the same time, their presence in the country may only benefit a small segment of the population while worsening everyone else's situation.

Labour relations and supplier controls

Considerations here include the "hiring and firing" of staff, wage policies, overtime, health and safety, gender equality, child labour, union relations and fair trade. The enormous global variability of labour market conditions makes it difficult to assume a standardisation of MNE ethics in this domain.

Corruption

Corruption skews market transactions to the benefit of the few and detriment of the many. The problem is the extreme global variation in levels of perceived corruption (a quantum best tracked in an index designed by a Vienna-based NGO called Transparency International). Depending on a country's cultural heritage, practices considered corrupt in some environments (political lobbying, gifts) may be acceptable and even seen as normal in others.

Environment

Issues here include ascertaining MNEs' responsibilities and willingness to clean up existing pollution, prevent further pollution and conserve natural resources. Where ecological problems are limited to one country, its government can try to police the company involved by applying a "polluter pays" principle. The problem is that ecological damage often knows no borders, making it harder to attribute responsibility and police the problem especially in the absence of an all-powerful international authority with cross-border jurisdiction.

International codes of conduct

There have been many attempts over the years to codify ethical behaviour on an international scale. The two main categories are efforts made by the United Nations (UN) and voluntary codes drafted by companies.

UN conventions

The UN is the closest thing the world has to a global government. It falls far short of fulfilling this role, however, due to a lack of policing powers and because its decisions require consensus agreement from members whose interests often differ. Having said that, there is still value in reviewing some of the UN's main recent agreement.

1   1992 UN Rio de Janeiro Conference on Environment and Development

Building on seminal work that the Norwegian politician Gro Brundtland undertook in the field of "sustainable development,", this was the first "Earth Summit" where world leaders assembled to "rethink economic development and find ways to halt the destruction of irreplaceable natural resources and pollution of the planet".

2   1997 UN Kyoto Framework Convention on Climate Change

The convention set "an overall framework for intergovernmental efforts to tackle the challenge posed by climate change". Its effectiveness was undermined when several major polluter countries refused to ratify it. Subsequent climate change conferences (including the 2019 Madrid COP25) have run into similar difficulties.

3   2000 UN Global Compact (see Figure 4.2)

Human Rights
Principle 1: Businesses should ...support and respect the protection of internationally proclaimed human rights; and
Principle 2: ...make sure that they are not complicit in human rights abuses.
Labour Standards
Principle 3: Businesses should uphold ...the freedom of association and the effective recognition of the right to collective bargaining;
Principle 4: ...the elimination of all forms of forced and compulsory labour;
Principle 5: ...the effective abolition of child labour; and
Principle 6: ...the elimination of discrimination in respect of employment and occupation.
Environment
Principle 7: Businesses should ...support a precautionary approach to environmental challenges;
Principle 8: ...undertake initiatives to promote greater environmental responsibility; and
Principle 9: ...encourage the development and diffusion of environmentally friendly technologies
Anti-Corruption
Principle 10: Businesses should work against all forms of corruption, including extortion and bribery

Figure 4.2 Principles of the UN Global Compact.

Members sign up to indicate their support for the Compact's principles. With more than 12,000 members in over 160 countries as of June 2020, this is probably the world's biggest voluntary CSR network.

4   2005 United Nations Convention Against Corruption (UNCAC)

The problem is that the only authorities with real power to punish corrupt companies are national governments applying domestic legislation. In the absence of sanctions, international codes can lack effectivenesss.

5   2019 Centenary International Labour Conference

Adoption of ILO Convention 190 Concerning the Elimination of Violence and Harassment in the World of Work. The perceived need to officialise these basic aspirations raises the question of whether voluntary and/or self-enforced codes of MNE ethics actually suffice.

Voluntary codes

Companies like to publicise the fact that they have drafted a code of ethical conduct, or signed up to an existing one, since this improves their reputation and defuses possible criticism.

Two of the world's biggest ethical reporting groups, after the UN Global Compact, are the Global Reporting Initiative (GRI) and the SA8000. The GRI is a large, "multi-stakeholder network" of experts promoting triple bottom line disclosure within a "Sustainability Reporting Framework". The SA 8000 is a "Social Accountability Standard" and verification system aimed at "assuring humane workplaces".

Otherwise, many business sectors have devised their own international codes of conduct. Examples include the International Council of Toy Industries and the International Code of Conduct on the Distribution and Use of Pesticides. As for branch-level codes, these tend focus as much on labour practices and product safety as on environmental standards.

Also noteworthy at this level is the rise of environmental and/or social ratings agencies (like MSCI in the United States or BMJ in France) that promote ethical practice – much in the same way as financial ratings agencies like Moody's or Standard and Poor's improve corporate governance (another component of business ethics) by maximising financial disclosure.

Lastly, a fast-growing area of ethical codification is fair trade, where certification is largely overseen by an entity called FLO International.

This sector began with attempts to create products (like Fair Trade Coffee and Rugmark carpets) whose entire branding is based on the application of ethical business practices, mainly revolving around raw material producers being paid above-market prices to ensure they receive a "living wage". Fair trade certification then becomes a badge that some consumers will specifically seek in the stores where they go shopping making this sector one of the purest examples of CSR turned into a profit strategy.

Enforcing CSR worldwide

It is one thing to specify which ethical standards MNEs should adopt. It is another to enforce actual implementation. Ethical behaviour is easier to identify within a national framework where everyone answers to a single authority (the national government). This is not the case in many MNE dealings.

National traditions of CSR enforcement

CSR materialises across the world in different forms. In the US, for instance, firms may feel greater pressure to offer concrete evidence that they are operating ethically. This can be partly explained by the fact that before the Sarbanes–Oxley corporate governance bill became law in 2002, limited liability meant that US executives could often avoid personal responsibility for their actions at work. In an environment where accountability is less formalised, overt CSR actions reassure the public and can be marketed as a new competitive tool.

Europe, on the other hand, is marked by a tradition of strong legal prescriptions, exemplified by Germany's concept of *Eigentum verpflichtet* (loosely translated as "Ownership creates duties"). Note as well the increasingly widespread adoption of triple bottom line legislation, exemplified by France's 2001 *Nouvelles Régulations Economiques*, which require most firms to publish environmental and social accounts alongside their financial statements.

Japan's CSR profile translates the country's largely collective culture in which the search for social harmony – an Asian cultural value enshrined in the writings of the philosopher Confucius – takes precedence over self-interest. Interestingly, many poor countries in Asia share similar values to Japan without CSR being as prevalent as it is there. This offers further proof that a society's attitudes towards business ethics is conditioned by multiple factors, including stage of socioeconomic development.

The clear priority in many emerging economies has been to create jobs and spark growth by attracting inward investment. As Chapter 12 will detail, one common feature in much of the Global South is the absence of sufficiently strong civil institutions to exert moral pressure on companies. Corruption is rife, often because living standards are so low that potential recipients of bribes cannot afford to turn their backs on potential sources of income. The net effect is that in some parts of the world, CSR seems a luxury. At the same time, it is patently unfair that the world's poorest nations should suffer worse corporate behaviour than their wealthier counterparts.

Market policing: non-governmental organisations (NGOs) and consumers

One rapidly expanding feature of the international business ethics landscape is NGOs' use of high-profile communications campaigns to influence how consumers view MNEs. Much of the time, this involves denouncing MNEs that engage in unethical behaviour or refuse responsibility for their actions' damaging consequences. NGOs' public exposure of MNE behaviour is intended to attract the attention of politicians and legislators (in the hope they will intervene) as well as consumers (in the hope they will threaten commercial boycotts). It explains why NGOs might well be categorised as a new power base helping to define international business ethics today.

The effectiveness of NGO protests as a vehicle for enforcing ethical behaviour remains to be seen, however. MNEs are not going to agree to any and all protestor demands – if only because the benefits of unethical behaviour may be higher than the costs of compliance with legal and/or CSR standards. This is especially true when the misconduct is happening far away from the MNE's main consumer markets. The debate then becomes to what extent a company whose representatives behave ethically in certain locations should be blamed for colleagues' past or present misconduct elsewhere. This is a complicated subject. Few MNEs – like few human beings – are 100% ethical or unethical.

Bibliography

Carson, T. (1993), "Friedman's Theory of Corporate Social Responsibility", *Business and Professional Ethics Journal*, Volume 12, No. 1 (Spring), pp. 3–32.

Chun, R. (2019), "How Virtuous Global Firms Say They Are: A Content Analysis of Ethical Values", *Journal of Business Ethics*, Volume 155, No. 1, pp. 57–73.

Heath, E., Kaldis, B. and Marcoux, A. M. (eds) (2018), *The Routledge Companion to Business Ethics*, Abingdon: Routledge.

Hopkins, M. (2008), *Corporate Social Responsibility and International Development: Is Business the Solution?*, Abingdon: Routledge.

Vogel, D. (2006), *The Market for Virtue: The Potential and Limits of Corporate Social Responsibility*, Washington (DC):Brookings Institute.

"What's great is that everyone gets along".

5 Cultural environments

Essential summary

This chapter looks at the role of culture in international business environments. It starts by examining and defining the components of culture, with a focus on language and religion. It then outlines the impact of culture on communication, leadership, and organisation, explaining why companies cannot afford to ignore cultural differences when operating across borders. Theories of culture – such as Hofstede's cultural dimensions and the cluster approach – can be used by international managers to better understand the cultural preferences of people (customers, staff, partners, suppliers) in different countries. The chapter concludes with the concept of cultural intelligence, which provides a framework for the development of cross-cultural competence among international managers.

With more than 7,100 languages spoken in the world, it is understandable that international managers may struggle to communicate effectively across borders with their counterparts. Language and culture are indissociable. Both shape people's world view and reflect their values and beliefs.

The term culture refers to the long-standing and implicit shared values, beliefs, customs, artefacts and other products of human thoughts and work that characterise members of a given group or society. Given the extent of globalisation, international managers cannot afford to ignore differences in taste (customers), leadership styles (staff management) or expressions of national traditions and customs in their target markets. Failure to do so may prove damaging for the success of their overseas operations. Indeed, cross-cultural management is one of the four major risks faced by companies operating across borders, alongside commercial, currency, and political/country risks.

As an example, the Society for Human Resources Management (SHRM) reports that more than 30% of international M&A fail due to cultural differences. International business practitioners rarely if ever ask whether cultural diversity matters – because it clearly does. The question is what to do about it.

Culture and its impact on international business

The components of culture

The key components of culture include language and religion, which help alongside other factors to determine the values, attitudes, customs and norms of a group and/or society as a whole. How these factors interact is complex, as is the whole concept of culture, which is simultaneously visible and invisible, tacit and implicit, stable and evolutive. The cultural iceberg (Figure 5.1) is a common metaphor used to illustrate that understanding culture requires international managers to seek information beyond the visible and observable elements of culture. It emphasises the idea that the most influential aspects of culture lie below

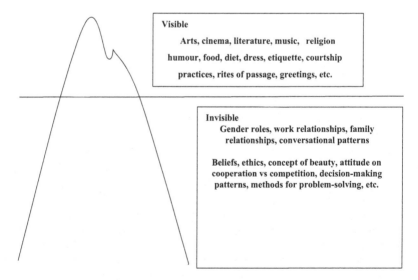

Visible

Arts, cinema, literature, music, religion

humour, food, diet, dress, etiquette, courtship

practices, rites of passage, greetings, etc.

Invisible
Gender roles, work relationships, family
relationships, conversational patterns

Beliefs, ethics, concept of beauty, attitude on
cooperation vs competition, decision-making
patterns, methods for problem-solving, etc.

Figure 5.1 The cultural iceberg.

the surface and are therefore more difficult to decipher – especially values, beliefs, attitudes, and social norms.

Language

Cross-cultural communication refers to the ways in which people from different cultural backgrounds communicate and create shared meaning. With the rise in global trade and international supply chains, effective cross-cultural communication has become an imperative for companies managing a diverse workforce or conducting business across borders. Thus, MNEs increasingly acknowledge that cross-cultural communication and collaboration are crucial for their financial success overseas. Over the years, studies have repeatedly shown that MNE CEOs and HR managers consider language barriers and cultural differences to be a leading cause of the challenges they face when entering new foreign markets. Despite acknowledging the role of effective cross-cultural communication, international companies often fail to take action and integrate intercultural competence and language skills into their training programmes or recruitment processes. This is further emphasised by a common misconception that modern technology in the form of emails, instant messaging, or online meeting platforms can alleviate cross-cultural differences and misunderstandings.

Another common assumption is that all people involved in international business speak English, hence there is no point learning foreign languages or about other cultures. The fact today is that Chinese, Spanish, Hindi, and Arabic speakers represent more than a third of the global population. English is used as an international business language (referred to as *lingua franca*); however most English speakers have learned it as a second or third language. Consequently, the level of fluency in English may vary, the net effect being that international business practitioners will sometimes refrain from critical discussion in meetings because they feel they cannot explain themselves with subtlety and accuracy. Sometimes business jargon and idiomatic expressions may cause communication issues. A non-native English speaker may be puzzled by phrases like "bottom line" or "beat around the bush". Even native English speakers may face some difficulties in understanding one another. Differences in meaning between American and British English are also numerous – one example being the word "trainers", which signifies jogging in British English ("sneakers" in American English), not to refer to the people who deliver training in organisations (often called "consultants" or "coaches"). Lastly, non-verbal communication across cultures may also create confusion. For example, Bulgarians and Indian people use a head shake movement to show their interest, respect, and understanding of the message conveyed by their interlocutor. This could easily lead to cross-cultural misunderstandings in meetings where participants read such clues inaccurately.

Religion

Ethical values, managerial practices, working patterns, customs and food are highly influenced by religion. Whether they are religious or not, it is important for international managers to understand the different belief systems institutionalised in foreign countries. Christianity accounts for approximately two billion worshippers, while Islam accounts for 1.5 billion, and Hinduism and Buddhism account for one billion each. Other religious and belief systems include Confucianism and Judaism. The World Economic Forum provides an updated global map of the world's major religions, which is particularly useful for international managers. It shows that Christianity dominates in the Americas, Europe and the southern half of Africa. Islam is the primary religion in a group of countries spanning from northern Africa through the Middle East to Indonesia. The largest Hindu community can be found in India, and China has the world's largest 'atheist/agnostic' population. Buddhism is the majority religion in South-East Asia and Japan.

Notwithstanding current debates on the positive and/or negative effects of religion on economic growth, some people continue to affirm that religious affiliations help create bonds of trust and shared commitment, which facilitate exchange of goods and services across borders.

Socialisation and acculturation

Culture is a collective phenomenon which outlines the shared values, norms and behaviours of a group or society. However, individual variation may occur as people do not always behave according to the dominant cultural framework. Also, the rise in migration and self-initiated expatriation suggest that individuals may live and work in various cultural environments over the course of their lives. As a result, international managers can develop a multifaceted cultural identity and feel that they belong not to one national culture but to a cosmopolitan community. Assuming that an employee will behave according to his/her country's cultural framework may result in misinterpretation and stereotyping. Yet it is also likely that a manager born and raised in Spain, for instance, will share some characteristics with Spaniards. Managers should therefore learn about cultural hybrids and be open to individual variations when managing staff at a global level.

Socialisation

Socialisation refers to the process of enculturation whereby people learn the rules and behavioural patterns deemed appropriate in their society. This starts usually within their family unit. The process of adjusting and adapting to a culture other than one's own is called acculturation.

International managers may have been exposed to multiple cultures as children, students, and professionals. Drawing on the socio-constructivist paradigm, their cultural identity could be interpreted as having been forged by their social interactions, including those with family, friends, teachers, mentors, colleagues and managers, who may (or may not) come from different cultural backgrounds than the manager's own.

National, professional, and corporate cultures

People experience progressive socialisation during their life: first in their country (national), then in their occupational environment (professional), and then in their organisation (corporate). The medical, military, and academic professions, for instance, hold very distinctive sets of norms, values and behaviours, often regulated by professional bodies and institutions. The same might be said about the international business community. At an organisational level, some companies (like Google, for instance) are known for their flexibility, fun and sense of employee ownership. By contrast, some others (like Tesla possibly) are associated with entrepreneurship and a risk-taking approach to business, being an extension of their founder's style (in this case, Elon Musk). Hence, a global corporate culture may grow to prevail over national cultural preferences.

The co-existence of the three layers of culture – national, professional, and organisational – presents an additional challenge to international managers, namely which one is likely to have a predominant effect on employee behaviour. Some answers to this question might be found in the concept of cultural relativity. In anthropology, cultural relativity (or relativism) claims that individuals can only be understood in the context of their own culture. In other words, one can only appreciate a culture using its own cultural frame of reference, similar to

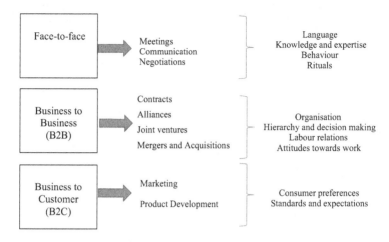

Figure 5.2 Impact of culture in different business contexts.

a pair of glasses through which a person sees the world. Consequently, international managers are often advised to refrain from judging a situation or behaviour based on the standards of their own culture; instead, it is deemed more useful to learn the standards of the other culture and develop a contextual interpretation of their observations from this. Of course, the question then becomes whether the international manager actually follows this piece of advice or not.

All in all, doing business across borders not only involves financial calculation but also personal relationships where trust and common interests prevail. Cross-cultural management focuses on three dimensions that are critical to international business: communication, leadership and organisation. Cross-cultural differences affect four main aspects of international business transactions: cultural differences; negotiation patterns; decision-making styles; and ethical practices. The extent of culture's impact on different international business contexts is summarised in the figure above (Figure 5.2).

Theories of culture for international business

International managers can refer to theories and frameworks to better understand the culture of their foreign counterparts and use this to adapt their management style and internationalisation strategy. There are two main approaches to culture in international business: the dimension approach and the cluster approach. Whichever applies, it is important to note that there are no right or wrong aspects of culture; all cultural dimensions have advantages and drawbacks in a business context. They also only represent a general trend, and variations can be found in the range of behaviours seen as appropriate in a given culture.

The main model exploring cultural dimensions is one developed by Dutch social psychologist Geert Hofstede's. Learners with a particular interest in culture within international business can also benefit by engaging in further research of two other leading constructs: Fons Trompenaars's dimensions (e.g. universalism *vs* particularism; individualism *vs* collectivism) and Edward T. Hall's contextual approach (e.g. low *vs* high context).

Hofstede's cultural dimensions

Geert Hofstede pioneered research on culture with a seminal study conducted on IBM employees in 64 countries between 1967 and 1973, with further countries and data having been added since this time. Hofstede's output constitutes what has come to be considered one of the most comprehensive studies of how values in the workplace are influenced by culture. Six cultural levels or dimensions emerged from the findings and are presented below.

Individualism vs collectivism

This dimension describes whether a person serves and performs primarily as an individual or as part of a group. Individualistic societies (e.g. Australia, Canada, the US, the UK) typically value self-interest and competition for resources over alignment with a group. By contrast, collectivistic societies (e.g. China and South Korea) value strong ties between individuals and view life as a cooperative experience; conformity and compromise are viewed here as paramount to maintaining harmony.

Power distance

This dimension refers to the level of egalitarianism and deference to authority in a society. In high power distance cultures (e.g. Russia, Venezuela), superiors and senior managers are treated with deference and vertical hierarchy is respected. In low power distance cultures (e.g. Australia, the US, Denmark), relationships at work are more egalitarian, with a loose and horizontal approach to organisational structure.

Masculine vs feminine

This dimension outlines how a society appreciates attributes traditionally associated with men (assertiveness, competition, emphasis on quantitative measures of success) or women (modesty, caring for others, emphasis on qualitative measures of success). However, it is important to note that it does not refer to the position of women in society nor to gender equality. Denmark, Sweden, and Norway are described as feminine cultures, whereas Japan, Greece, and Mexico are identified as masculine cultures.

Uncertainty avoidance

This refers to people's attitude towards risk and uncertainty in their lives. For example, in Belgium, France and Japan, which score high on uncertainty avoidance, people may expect institutions to regulate the market and minimise financial risk. Also, individuals may aspire to a stable and clear career plan. By contrast, countries with low uncertainty avoidance, such as India, Ireland, Jamaica and the US, value risk-taking, a quick decision-making process and entrepreneurial managers.

Time orientation

Long-term and short-term cultural orientations refer to the emphasis on short-run or long-run sense of temporality and success. People and organisations with a long-term orientation plan years and decades ahead. Asian societies, including China, Japan and Singapore, typically value this long-term approach to success, based upon the principles of the Chinese philosopher Confucius. Conversely, most Western countries have a more short-term orientation.

Indulgence vs restraint

This sixth dimension was added to the framework in 2010. It refers to people's attitudes towards happiness and how they try to control their desires and impulses. In indulgent societies, employees may feel more inclined to share their emotions, express opinions, give feedback, and move jobs (e.g. the US, Sweden, Mexico). By contrast, the happiness of an individual may be less valued in restrained societies (China, Egypt, Russia) where strict social norms typically dictate people's behaviour. Thus, individuals may be reluctant to express their needs and display emotions. Also, career and job mobility may be perceived as limited or constrained.

The cluster approach

International managers navigating across cultures may be confused by the extent of differences the national and regional variations they encounter. Clusters are useful in providing a framework underlining cultural similarities instead of differences. Also, this approach can be used to substantiate similar marketing and management strategies in a specific group of countries.

The Global Leadership and Organisational Behaviour Effectiveness (GLOBE) project proposes six regional groupings of 61 countries based on nine cultural dimensions: Latin Europe, Eastern Europe, Germanic Europe, Arabic, Anglo, and Southern Asia.

The study reveals, for instance, that Germanic Europe (Austria, Germany, the Netherlands, and German Switzerland) is the most risk-averse cluster. Similarly, Eastern Europe (Albania, Georgia, Greece, Hungary, Kazakhstan, Poland, Russia, and Slovenia) avoids uncertainty in favour of stability in a business context. These are culture-based attitudes that can have a direct international business effect, one example being the size of the equity investment that MNEs from one or the other of these groups are willing to make in a cross-border acquisition.

Limitations of these two approaches

The cluster approach is often criticised for overgeneralising the cultural traits of numerous countries. Based on a Western paradigm of culture, the grouping of countries in clusters may itself be culturally biased.

Otherwise, Hofstede's model of culture is well-known and widely used in organisations but has some limitations of its own. Firstly, the study was originally based on data collected in a single company, IBM; hence it may be difficult to generalise its findings. Secondly, although multiple updates and regular reviews have occurred since the 1970s, the study may be outdated, considering the extent of economic, social, political and technological changes at local, regional and global levels. Third, the method used to collect the data was mainly quantitative, in the form of a questionnaire, which is not as effective in exploring the deep meaning of a phenomenon such as culture. Nevertheless, Hofstede's work has contributed greatly to raising awareness of the impact of culture in international business. It provides a useful guide helping to foster international managers' cross-cultural competence.

Optimising assignments abroad

Expatriate assignments may result in success or failure, depending on employees' readiness to relocate abroad. Studies have shown that up to 70% of expatriations fail in the Global South and up to 45% fail in the Global North. Others estimate the annual cost of failed overseas assignments in American MNEs, for instance, at $2 billion. Business-related consequences include damaged client relations and issues with suppliers, partners and governments. The impact on human resources is also worth considering since talented international managers may suffer from low self-esteem, resentment and eventually disengagement from their organisation. The selection, preparation, and management of expatriates requires further attention, although this is not usually considered a priority in MNEs.

Culture shock

When exposed to a foreign culture, expatriates are likely to experience culture shock, defined as sequential reactions induced by their immersion in a new, unpredictable and uncertain environment. There are typically four stages of culture shock. First, the anticipation stage, which may generate both excitement and anxiety prior to departure overseas. Second, a honeymoon period, which may occur when the expatriate discovers their new environment with excitement and enjoyment. Third, a frustration phase due to cross-cultural management issues and miss their home country, family and friends. Fourth, the period of normalisation, where they succeed in making new friends, get used to a new lifestyle and find ways to work effectively in the new environment. The role of family is pivotal in making the expatriation assignment a success. As a result, MNEs increasingly include partners and children in cross-cultural communication and language training in preparation for an overseas assignment. Still, about one-third of MNEs fail to provide this support on the basis that many appointments are made too rapidly to allow for in-depth preparation.

Another point worth considering is the repatriation process, whereby expatriates return to their home country. The question becomes what position, role, pay, social status, and career they will hold there and whether friends still be there for them, (and relate to them) after their "exotic" experience abroad. Expatriates may experience reverse culture shock and may need some time to re-adjust to their home country upon return.

Managing diverse teams

Although cultural diversity generates innovation and creativity in organisations, cross-cultural conflicts may arise and hinder the productivity and effectiveness of multicultural teams. Three approaches can be used by international managers to deal with these issues. They can adopt the cultural norms and values of their home country, which, in turn, will shape the firm's global corporate culture (ethnocentric). Conversely, they may adopt the cultural norms and preferences of the company's host country (polycentric). Lastly, they can develop a context-sensitive approach by selecting the best of both cultures to achieve success (geocentric). These approaches are further discussed in Chapter 11.

Developing cultural intelligence

Cultural intelligence or cultural quotient (CQ) describes the capability to recognise and function effectively with people from a different cultural background or in different cultural contexts. Research has shown that cultural intelligence can be developed and measured by taking a CQ assessment. No one is competent in all cultural contexts. Yet the capacity to understand and adapt one's behaviour in complex cultural settings requires four CQ capabilities:

CQ drive: motivation to interact with people from different cultural backgrounds;
CQ knowledge: cognitive capacity and knowledge on cultural dimensions, values, social norms, languages and religions;
CQ strategy: social-cognitive capacity to make sense of cross-cultural experiences;
CQ action: ability to adapt verbal and non-verbal communication and adopt appropriate behaviours in different cultural settings.

MNEs increasingly seek employees who can demonstrate a global mindset and a capacity to adapt quickly to diverse cultural environments. However, learning a new language or experiencing total immersion in a foreign culture may necessitate several months of study and practice. International managers are usually not given much time to prepare for an assignment overseas. Hence, students and young professionals who dream of a global career may instead opt for study abroad schemes at university, international internships and/or language training. This will make them stand out from the crowd and propel their careers to new heights.

Bibliography

Beugelsdijk, S., Kostova, T. and Roth, K. (2017), "An Overview of Hofstede-Inspired Country-level Culture Research in International Business since 2006", *Journal of International Business Studies*, Volume 48, pp. 30–47.

Eberhard, D. M., Simons, G. F. and Fennig, C. D. (eds) (2020), *Ethnologue: Languages of the World*, 23rd edition, Dallas, Texas: SIL International, available at http://www.ethnologue.com, last accessed: 27/02/2020.

Meyer, E. (2015), *The Culture Map: Decoding How People Think, Lead, and Get Things Done Across Cultures*, Public Affairs: New York.

Tietze, S., Michailova, S. and Holden, N. (2015), *The Routledge Companion to Cross-Cultural Management*, Routledge: London.

Weisheit, J. (2018) "Should I Stay, or Should I Go? A Systematic Literature Review about the Conceptualization and Measurement of International Relocation Mobility Readiness", *Journal of Global Mobility*, Volume 6, No. 2, pp. 129–157.

"How we supposed to get in there?"

6 Foreign market entry

Essential summary

With the exception of a few firms that were "born-globals", most of the world's leading MNEs grew up in a home market where they were able to achieve the critical mass they felt was necessary before venturing abroad. This means that at one point in time, each had to make a conscious decision to internationalise – with the question then becoming how (see Figure 6.1) and why they made the decisions they did. Analysis here involves both the strategic elements typifying each kind of market entry mode as well as more subjective factors like managers' "commitment to internationalisation" and attitudes towards cross-border risk.

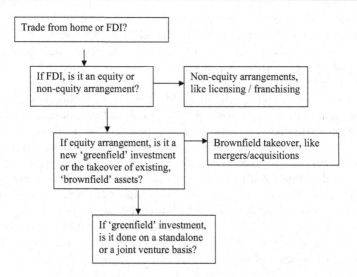

Figure 6.1 Ladder of internationalisation choices.

Internationalisation mindsets and strategies

Prime theories

The seminal construct in international business studies is Swedish professors Johanson and Vahlne's famous "Uppsala model", which views foreign expansion as a gradual learning process where firms only commit resources abroad as they become accustomed to working in new environments. This "stages of internationalisation" approach predicts that managers first cross borders via trade modes committing fewer resources – simple import or export contracts – before engaging in Foreign Direct Investment (FDI) modes, which require a greater commitment of assets and therefore entail greater risk. The model also assumes that managers tend to prefer that their company's first move abroad be to a neighbouring country characterised by a lesser "psychic distance" from their home market – and that it is only once they have developed confidence in their ability to operate internationally (and process previous experiences) that they will venture even further afield.

The key factor here is the variability of human reactions to the uncertainty associated with the relative "foreignness" of a given environment. Uppsala views international business decision-making as highly subjective. Hence its focus on practitioners' risk attitudes and mindsets ("domestic" or "global"), with company size being another relevant factor.

Other theories place greater emphasis on more strategic thinking. Network theory, derived from work done by American sociologist Mark Granovetter, infers for instance that it is actors' desire to link into a powerful cluster of activities that drives behaviour such as internationalisation. In this view, more objective factors like business potential have greater weight than the subjective risk attitudes highlighted in Uppsala theory. Otherwise, there is the value chain approach – largely constructed on the back of insights formulated by the economist Alfred Marshall – asking whether a MNE seeks to reduce uncertainty by engaging in the same sorts of activities abroad as at home (so-called horizontal internationalisation) or else pursues "vertical" integration by controlling different upstream or downstream activities overseas. Lastly, "transaction cost" analysis, based on theories developed by economists like Oliver Williamson, view market entry decisions as attempts to minimise the costs of locating different value chain activities in different countries – an approach which includes consideration of the fact that for companies operating in geographically isolated and/or saturated (hence low-margin) home markets, the decision not to internationalise may be the riskiest of all.

Trade *vs* **FDI**, *or the "borders of the firm" debate*

The easiest way to engage in international business is not to change the business "configuration" (what it does where) and simply trade from home, that is, import inputs from foreign suppliers or export outputs to foreign customers. This keeps a company focused on its tried and tested core competencies and frees it from having to develop international manufacturing, sales or logistics capabilities.

A decision to enter foreign markets via trade as opposed to FDI might also be a reflection of the general paradigms underlying executives' action. The main debate here is between a "small is beautiful" willingness to outsource some activities to (foreign) specialists capable of performing them better and/or more cheaply versus the argument that companies should maximise control and internalise value chain margins by doing everything themselves via FDI. Viewed in this light, internationalising via trade is an example of a construct developed by British economist Ronald Coase where managers draw narrower "boundaries of the firm" (see Figure 6.2). Note that this calculation can be based on financial considerations (with import/export becoming an interesting option if FDI costs are higher than the value added that the trade-only MNE would otherwise share with foreign suppliers and/or vendors) but also on psychological factors (executives' risk-averse preference for limited intervention).

Of course, where companies' only internationalisation involves trading with other value chain intermediaries, they become dependent on the latter, something that can cause problems. Import/export contracts might be incomplete and not cover certain troublesome scenarios (bad quality, unreliable deliveries, late payments). There is also the risk that

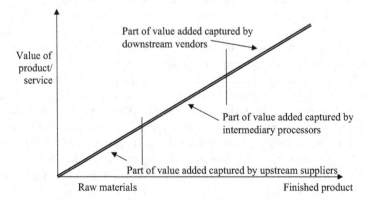

Figure 6.2 Value added and the boundaries of the firm.

an opportunistic supplier or vendor might appropriate the company's know-how and expand its own operations up or down the value chain to become a direct competitor.

Horizontal *vs* vertical FDI

This explains many firms' preference for internationalising via FDI, whose flows account directly today for anything between 3% and 5% of global GDP, vs. less than 1% before the early 1990s. As aforementioned, one key delineation at this level is whether the FDI is horizontal in nature and therefore involve a relatively straightforward transfer of knowledge from one country to another, or if it is vertical, with the MNE incurring the risk of having to develop a new kind of activity in a new environment. Horizontal FDI tends to dominate in high-tech sectors where protecting the confidentiality of a company's intellectual property is paramount. Having said that, it also costs more since it duplicates activities on several sites. Moreover, output from an MNE's horizontal plants will tend to reduce exports from its existing units, affecting the latter's economies of scale.

On the other hand, these are losses only felt by the MNE's individual plants – at the broader level of the company as a whole, horizontal FDI can increase economies of scale due to the fact that many assets (especially intangible ones) will not in fact have to be reproduced everywhere. This goes a long way towards paying horizontal FDI's duplication of overheads.

Vertical FDI, on the other hand, will often see a company build specialist "focused factories" in different countries, with each engaged in just one specific value chain activity. The advantage of this configuration is that each unit benefits from the competitive advantages inherent to its location, thereby achieving site-specific economies of scale and learning. More and more internationalisation is based on this intra-firm logic today, with MNEs' "offshoring" of various functions culminating in in-house units trading with one another up and down the value chain.

The downside for MNEs with this configuration is that increased shipments between international sites raise "trade costs" like packaging, transit time, freight and tariffs. Some MNEs try to reduce these costs by focusing production on fewer sites, mainly ones with good transport links to the plants where the final product will be assembled. At a certain juncture, however, managers may decide that vertical integration's overall trade costs exceed the benefits. They may then transition to "vertical disintegration", drawing the boundaries of their own firm more narrowly and increasing trade with external partners instead of the offshore units owned by the MNE itself. This logic has been a key factor driving the decades-long explosion in international outsourcing (see Chapter 8), with some studies indicating that intermediate goods have accounted for something like 60% of all global trade in recent years.

Market entry choices

Even after an MNE decides to build up foreign presence, it retains a number of options. Many companies, especially SMEs but also larger MNEs uncomfortable with a given environment, will start with a small representative office, adding organisational learning about the location before risking resources there.

Where companies opt for full-blown FDI, the first decision is whether to build new "greenfield" facilities or acquire existing "brownfield" assets. This choice is often referred to as the "build or buy" dilemma.

Greenfield *vs* brownfield

The first delineation between these two modes is that greenfield FDI tends to be preferable when a company prioritises technological confidentiality, due to the fact that knowledge can be transferred internally from the MNE's existing sites to the new location, making it easier to achieve "first-mover" advantage in the new country. A brownfield mode, on the other hand, is usually deemed more appropriate where the internationalisation is driven by commercial objectives (since it is easier and quicker to penetrate the new market when the effort is led by a unit that is already up and running).

In terms of the "build or buy" dilemma, the advantage of greenfield FDI is that it causes companies to spend much less time and money identifying and acquiring an appropriate target – assuming that one even exists. They also avoid the goodwill costs associated with purchasing an existing asset. Brownfield FDI, on the other hand, is fast since it avoids start-up problems inherent to any new venture – a prospect that is particularly attractive when the new country differs greatly from the ones to which the MNE is accustomed. Brownfield modes also offer the possibility of benefiting from the brand reputation of the company that is being acquired as well as its existing customer base. Lastly, by taking over an existing producer, the MNE is not adding to a sector's total production capacities and thereby increasing global supply – the effect of which would be to lower market prices, undermining the company's own interests as a producer.

International mergers and acquisitions (M&A) constitute a prime example of brownfield FDI. Consolidations of this sort tend to happen in waves, reflecting managers' conformism to whatever sectorial paradigm happens to dominate at a certain point in time – a real-life application of anthropologist René Girard's "mimetic theory".

The justification for an international M&A can be a sales-side argument like a new market ("forward integration") or a production-side motive like access to resources ("backward integration"). Within these frameworks, the underlying aspiration is to achieve synergies by uniting companies with complementary geographic, product and/or technological capabilities – an approach that seems to have translated in recent years into fewer but much bigger international "mega-deals", amounting to $3.7 trillion in 2019. Having said that, the downside is that after the M&A finalises, managers generally face an enormous task ensuring that the new combined teams function harmoniously. The potential for discord between new colleagues coming from very different parts of the world – hence characterised by very different business cultures and ambitions – is a key factor shaping MNE thinking about the best way to internationalise.

International partnerships

Given the complication of operating in environments very different from the one(s) to which an MNE is accustomed, many managers see benefits in internationalising together with partners who both offer knowledge about the new market in question and are willing to share the entry costs and risks. The problem here is the possibility that an MNE's international partners may ultimately act against its interests. According to American political scientist Francis Fukuyama, trust is a key differentiating factor in many international business decisions.

Depending on the length of time they have been designed to last, MNE partnerships are sometimes referred to as "strategic alliances". This can assume various forms, ranging from permanent M&As to limited one-off co-operations where companies share a specific function (R&D, logistics). To some extent, the choice at this level is whether the partnership involves equity capital or not – a reflection once again of the level of international risk that managers are willing to take.

International joint ventures

International joint ventures (IJVs) are equity arrangements where an MNE and its partner each take a percentage stake in a new company, often built on a greenfield basis. The motivation tends to be managers' recognition that whereas FDI via wholly owned subsidiaries leaves a company with greater control and upside potential, MNEs may struggle to succeed on their own in complicated foreign environments.

MNEs will often seek host country IJV partners capable of fulfilling specific functions. This can involve staff recruitment or retention; supply chain operations; government interactions; and/or customer relationships. In turn, the incoming MNE is often expected to offer technological process and/or product expertise; access to international funding; and a recognisable brand name. The exact breakdown of partners' roles, along with the new venture's legal status (usually a partnership or limited liability company), depends on the counterparts' negotiating strengths but also on whether the IJV's aim is to sell into the host country or to use it as a manufacturing base for exports elsewhere.

Some IJVs are characterised by a 50–50 joint ownership. In others, one of the partners will have an at least 51% share, or even much higher. At times, this imbalance is voluntary and reflects one partner's desire for overall control. On other occasions, it is mandatory and reflects the host country government's requirement that domestic partners hold the dominant stake. This is especially true where the government deems the sector in which the IJV operates to be "strategic" to its national interest (e.g. military, banking, healthcare) or wants to maximise technology transfers. These political considerations help to explain why many partners agreeing IJV arrangements retain divergent objectives – being one reason why this market entry mode has such a high failure rate. The situation is complicated when IJV partners also compete outside of their arrangement, with neither wanting the other to benefit disproportionately.

All in all, the tensions that exist within IJVs mean that they are apt to under-perform other modes of market entry. IJVs' high failure rates have sparked much research on how to unwind them if and when they unravel. The easiest exit is for one partner to buy the other out but this is not always feasible and can cause further problems. In those instances where IJVs are too challenging and standalone FDI is too risky and expensive, companies need to consider other, less committed modes of internationalisation.

Non-equity arrangements

Companies that are hesitant about investing their own equity capital in a foreign venture can choose instead to share intangible assets (knowledge, brand name) with a local partner in exchange for the payment of fees and/ or royalties. These kinds of non-equity arrangements, called licensing or franchising contracts, are a common element in many MNEs' long-term market entry strategies. Other modes, like turnkey projects or management contracts, are more ad hoc in nature.

International licensing

There are basically two ways for firms to enforce private property rights. On one hand, where they own a particular process or item, they can sue anyone copying their intellectual property without permission in order to get the party to cease and, if possible, pay compensation. Conversely, they can proactively authorise another party to borrow their intellectual property rights, specifically because this helps them to enter a foreign market more quickly and above all at a lower cost. The legal term for this kind of authorisation is licensing, materialising in a contract between one party granting certain rights (the "licensor") and the other (the "licensee") receiving them.

Licensing contracts typically contain many specific clauses, starting with a precise definition of the product or process covered in the agreement but also including the geographic territory where it applies, its duration, the licensor's remuneration and any contract termination/renewal terms. International licensing agreements apply in many different areas but are often manufacturing-related.

International franchising

International franchising's rationale and contractualisation are similar to licensing but tend to focus more on downstream, commercial actions. A "franchisor" will sign a contract ("master license") with its local agent ("franchisee") granting the right to operate under its trade name and distribute its goods or services in a particular territory. To enable the franchisee to perform this function, the franchisor will typically provide all necessary support, including supplies, training, and advertising. The royalties it receives in return are often calculated as a percentage of the franchise's gross sales.

Many famous MNEs – often in the fast food sector (e.g. McDonald's or Subway) – have internationalised via this mode because it is quick and easy. Indeed, franchising is used in many sectors of activity worldwide. The advantage for the MNE is that it does not need to invest equity capital in overseas commercial outlets and can benefit from the local partner's experience in operating outlets and attracting local customers. The advantage for the franchisee is that it benefits from the international brand name and know-how of a company with a tried and tested business model.

Of course, like all market entry modes, licensing and franchising have their downsides. First, the royalties that an MNE receives may offer significant returns (especially since it was able to enter the market without putting up any equity capital) but are necessarily much lower than the potential profits from a wholly owned subsidiary. Second, certain specific risks are associated with international licensing/franchising. These include confidentiality (preventing industrial espionage); exclusivity (o keep the t partner from launching a rival operation one day); and performance (to ensure the materials that the partner uses, or the business practices it follows, do not damage the MNE's reputation).

The question then becomes how to control one's foreign partners. The contracts linking MNEs and their local agents must comply with legal conditions in the host country and be enforceable. This is easier to achieve if the MNE has a national presence staffed by individuals with knowledge of the local environment – an investment that is more justifiable where the MNE intends to commit to the host country, albeit on a non-equity basis, for the long run.

Turnkey projects

A final market entry category involves large scale one-off business opportunities. This is best exemplified by the kinds of infrequent but huge international contracts associated with particular sectors of activity, such as construction. Where a public infrastructure project is so big that no one company has the financial or technical resources to complete it alone, the order giver will often solicit an international "call for tender" from groups of companies organised into consortiums, inviting them to bid for the contract. Such consortia will usually have a prime contractor responsible for coordinating the tasks allocated to each participant. Partners in the consortium are contractually allied in the sense they work on the same overall project. At the same time, their ties are too ad hoc to justify an investment of equity capital. Once the project is completed, the consortium will be expected to hand over the keys to a fully functional system – and then disband. This explains why such arrangements are known as turnkey projects.

Bibliography

Granovetter, M. (1983), "The Strength of Weak Ties: A Network Theory Revisited", *Sociological Theory*, Volume 1, pp. 201–202.

Killing, P. (2003), "How to Make a Global Joint Venture Work", in Buckley, P. (ed.), *International Business*, Chapter 21, Routledge: Abingdon.

Rugman, A. (1982), *New Theories of the Multinational Enterprise*, Routledge: Abingdon.

Rugman, A. and Verbeke, A. (1992), "A Note on the Transnational Solution and the Transaction Cost Theory of Multinational Strategic Management", *Journal of International Business Studies*, 4th Quarter, 761–771.

Vahlne, J. and Johanson, J. (May 2013), "The Uppsala Model on Evolution of the Multinational Business Enterprise – From Internalization to Coordination of Networks", *International Marketing Review*, 30, 3, 189–210.

"Who did you say I'm reporting to?"

7 Multinational organisations and paradigms

Essential summary

Logically, Chapter 6's analysis of the way MNEs enter foreign markets should be followed by discussions of how they then manage whatever international configuration they then design. The topic is particularly poignant given how challenging it is to coordinate geographically and culturally diverse entities whose adherence to group objectives may be at odds with their need to fit into the local environment. In international business as in other social sciences, structures and mindsets influence one another.

MNE organisations

Theories about how MNEs organise and control their configurations tend to highlight the distribution of power between headquarters and subsidiaries – replicating to some extent the centre–periphery analysis that the sociologist Immanuel Wallerstein first formulated in his seminal world-systems approach. When applied to international business, the two extremes of this spectrum are a simple nation-by-nation orientation where subsidiaries enjoy maximal autonomy, versus a globalised orientation characterised by all-powerful headquarters.

Traditional divisions

In 1960, a young economist named Stephen Hymer wrote a seminal text analysing how companies approach FDI. According to Hymer, most MNEs begin life under the tight control of a few key managers working out of a single location. At this early stage, the company tends to view its first foreign missions as add-ons to existing operations. Specific offshore activities like trade documentation or logistics are separated from the company's existing structure and grouped into a new "international division". This structure may seem appropriate to firms who transact most of their business domestically. But it has the flaw of creating a mindset where the group executive under-estimates national specificities. Few MNEs opt for it today.

Hymer went on to assert that companies internationalise to exploit their monopoly advantages, often through vertical integration. Usually this means that the group executive takes responsibility for the cross-border implementation of strategy. In turn, this often results in a division-based structure known as the "Unitary (U-form)". For Hymer, this was the second organisational stage that MNEs implement once their capabilities reach a certain level.

The first configuration typifying second stage U-form MNEs is the "functional organisation", with each division responsible for a corporate function like manufacturing, marketing or finance. Here, it is the "centre" (head office) that controls the "periphery" (subsidiaries), whose mission is to implement strategies and technologies that senior management wants to implement. This mainly suits MNEs characterised by relatively undifferentiated product ranges. An MNE's main priority in this kind of structure is to ensure headquarters' operational control.

As the international business environment evolved over the course of the 20th century, Hymer detected a third organisational stage, called the "Multi-divisional (M-form)". To respond to global consumers' increasingly differentiated demands, MNEs need more flexible "product organisations" where each division acts as an independent profit centre. The goal here is to empower divisions to pursue their own product policies, depending on specific market conditions.

A widespread variant of the M-form structure among MNEs that view responsiveness as a priority is the "geographic organisation" (see Figure 7.1). Where consumer markets (or production conditions) vary widely from one country to another, it makes sense to empower frontline units with the most knowledge about local circumstances. The emphasis on international differentiation shifts power from the centre to the periphery, with group headquarters performing little more than simple resource allocation, performance control and strategic coordination missions.

The MNEs who push this logic to the extent of adopting a "multidomestic" paradigm in which each country is managed separately tend to be characterised by fragmented power structures. Greater responsiveness to local circumstances is a strength but also a weakness due to the

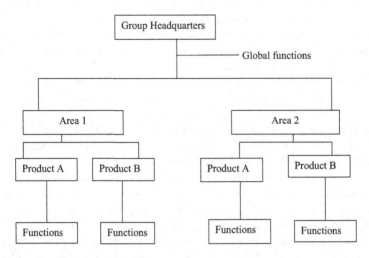

Figure 7.1 "Geographic" MNE organisation.

fact that it can blur headquarters' role and cause wasteful duplications, increasing overheads while making it harder to achieve group-wide economies of scale. Organisations of this kind also struggle to transfer knowledge between subsidiaries, with employees often communicating solely within their immediate unit and ignoring colleagues in other countries – all of which explains why many MNEs have abandoned the multi-domestic paradigm in recent years.

Global vs regional focus

By 1983, observers like Theodore Levitt were proclaiming the convergence of many international markets, particularly ones dominated by branded consumer goods. This meant that for MNEs in many sectors, what mattered was no longer differentiation along national lines but the ability to service global customers. Facing rivals who were increasingly sized to compete worldwide, firms needed to maximise their economies of scale. This called for an appropriate organisational configuration, one where the re-assertion of headquarters' power over subsidiaries would increase interdependency and maximise efficiency – explaining in turn many MNEs' renewed interest in functional or product organisations, as opposed to geographic ones.

Within a decade, however, a number of thought leaders would view the revival of globalised organisations in a more negative light. One critique was that it leaves little room for independent thinking at the local level. This had the effect of de-skilling subsidiaries and sparking resentment. There was also the risk that knowledge is only transmitted vertically, from headquarters to subsidiary or vice versa, undermining the possibility of subsidiary–subsidiary information flows. Lastly, where global organisations serve local markets from distant centralised manufacturing locations, they tend to suffer higher trade costs that can only be justified if these costs are less than the benefits derived from a centralisation of global production on just a few sites.

The new hybrid consensus in the 21st century is that it makes sense to centralise some functions (particularly upstream ones) while decentralising others (especially marketing, where proximity to end users is key). MNE decisions about where to locate which function depend on whether the priority is internal cohesion or external adaptation. Indeed, many MNEs juggle global and multi-domestic orientations simultaneously by adopting intermediary solutions – first and foremost, as pointed out notably in studies by international business professor Alan Rugman, being at the regional level.

As noted in United Nations Conference on Trade and Development (UNCTAD)'s Transnationality Index, many of the world's leading MNEs mostly do business within their home region. This means there is little advantage, hence incentive, for them to venture further abroad. Managers tend to feel more comfortable with a regulatory environment and general business culture that is more familiar to them – and where consumers resemble the ones they are in the habit of servicing. Transaction costs are also lower when companies operate closer to home. Indeed, much global production and R&D takes place in "clusters" organised along regional lines. In these cases, global headquarters usually do little more than oversee inter-regional transfers of assets and knowledge. The main power lies in the MNE's regional head office.

Transnational firms and glocalisation

The risk with any of these paradigms (multi-domestic, global or regional) is that they imprison MNEs in rigid structures of their own making. This has led to the argument, materialised in a seminal 1989 work published by international business researchers Christopher Bartlett and Sumantra Ghoshal (*Managing across Borders: A Transnational Solution*) that employee mindsets are just as crucial to an MNE's success as

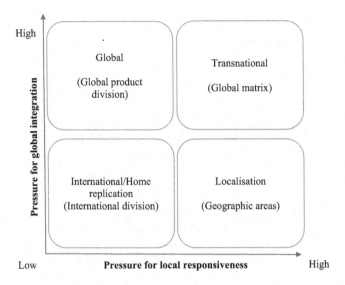

Figure 7.2 The integration-responsiveness framework.

official reporting lines. The idea here is that it does not matter whether strategies and innovation start in MNE headquarters or subsidiaries. The important thing is that staff be trained to apply global and/or local approaches (i.e. to "glocalise") as needs be – a hybrid approach that the authors called the "integration-responsiveness" (IR) paradigm, encapsulated in a four-side matrix that has over the years become one of the most famous and widely applied tools in all of international business (see Figure 7.2).

It is the hopefulness conveyed by IR that explains its popularity – the idea that MNE organisation and human capital can be used to overcome the fundamental contradiction at the heart of international business. By maximising both vertical (hierarchical) and horizontal (geographical) exchanges between all MNE units – a principle embodied in the "matrix organisation" that became popular in the 1990s – it spreads a gospel of flexibility that is very much in line with the contemporary zeitgeist. The idea here is that irrespective of people's unit of origin, there are many occasions when they should be temporarily allocated to an ad hoc team created to fulfil a specific task. The hope is that by encouraging multiple reporting lines and developing forums for information sharing, new synergies will arise, benefiting all product, function and geographic divisions. By itself, this has the potential for solving MNEs' permanent need to get useful information to the right people at the right time (see Figure 7.3).

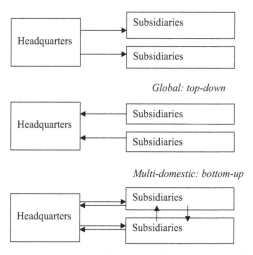

Figure 7.3 Power, strategy and information flows in different MNE paradigms.

At the same time, there is no doubt that the transnational paradigm also creates a serious organisational dilemma. Having to accumulate both global and local knowledge is both costly and time-consuming. Otherwise, some managers will struggle to combine cost efficiency with local responsiveness, especially when the value chain function they occupy relies predominantly on one of these factors and very little on the other. On top of this, asking staff to assume leadership roles in some situations but not in others raises questions about the permanence of MNE structures and the possibility for conflicting group *vs* subsidiary interests. Other problems are more cross-cultural in nature. Flexible structures are difficult to implement in the absence of flexible mindsets. With its multiple reporting lines and potential for information overload, a matrix organisation is often confusing and requires that staff work as organisational traffic controllers, identifying and re-directing colleagues' competencies. This is no easy task: the knowledge that a company holds is often very compartmentalised; and given the lack of trust that might reign between colleagues, especially from different locations, there may not be much enthusiasm for sharing. The uncertainty associated with matrix organisations and the transnational paradigm means that they are somewhat less widespread today than two decades ago.

MNEs as alliances of equals

In the end, the key to international success today may be a more balanced relationship between head offices and subsidiaries. What headquarters provide is overview and coordination. What subsidiaries offer is market awareness and, depending on their size, implementation capabilities. Moreover, because subsidiaries are in constant touch with suppliers and customers, their managers can be fertile sources of information, hence change drivers.

By hypothesizing that a firm is just as likely to accumulate advantage abroad as at home, the transnational paradigm is at odds with transaction cost theory, which assumes that most firm-specific advantages derive from an MNE's home country. It also contradicts resource-based theories rooted in the idea that resources and capabilities develop at the level of the firm as a whole. What it recognises instead is that different units contribute in different ways to overall performance – and that MNEs can be best understood as what UK academic Julian Birkinshaw has referred to as an "alliance of equals".

If MNE subsidiaries can create both power and knowledge, the real aim must be to ensure that these are disseminated through the company's "internal markets", being the succession of inhouse strategic business units that trade with one another up and down the value chain. In turn, this raises the question of which mission should be assigned to which unit. Things can get complicated if subsidiaries seeking to demonstrate their usefulness undermine fellow units. In this case, the centre's main authority over the periphery is to ensure fair competition among subsidiary managers. The human element, especially insofar as the management of knowledge is concerned, remains a key construct in MNE organisations.

Principles of multinational organisation

Some of the key variables that MNEs must consider before deciding upon a given type of organisation are strategic in nature. Others have more to do with the sociology of organisations – which plays out in a particular way where international business is concerned.

Strategic coherence

As aforementioned, certain strategic considerations necessarily argue in favour of certain MNE organisations. It would make no sense, for instance, to create, disseminate and exploit knowledge within divisions defined by geographic differentiation when an MNE offers a very narrow product range where the key factor of success is not diversity but instead the ability to enhance functional performance. Nor would it be logical to organise a company by products when the range it offers is so wide that knowledge about one product line could not possibly enhance the performance of another. In international like any other kind of business, coherence between strategy and structure is indispensable.

At times, this coherence relates to more objective factors. One such concept, often called "the institution-based view", refers to how well the MNE copes with whatever new socially embedded systems of rules it has encountered during its forays abroad. This can also be extended to its responses to changes in domestic or international political circumstances – one example being the way many European MNEs transitioned, following the 1993 implementation of the EU Single Market Rules, from multi-domestic approaches or geographic organisations highlighting market specificities to product or matrix organisations better able to integrate the diversity of the wider European national markets to which companies now had access. A second concept, called the "resource-based view" (RBV) – and particularly its VRIO (Value, Rarity, Imitability, Organisation) framework– zZfocuses on the value specifically generated by organisational decision-making. This is exemplified, for instance, by an MNE's locating a research centre in one country as opposed to another due to the former's special endowment in human capital, business networks and national innovation. Otherwise, RBV also envisions MNE organisation as having the ability to create rarity value which becomes another form of international competitive advantage – one example being when subsidiaries' approach to knowledge management causes them to develop particularly effective resource planning systems that differentiate them from rivals. Indeed, under RBV competitive advantage resides in MNEs' ability to create strong organisational structures juggling straightforward formal structures (policies, schemes, organisational charts) with more complex and less imitable informal ones (culture, ethics, teamwork, knowledge management systems). Where the MNE in question is large in size – hence hampered by flexibility constraints – but succeeds in applying these manoeuvres its competitive advantage will be commensurate to its organisational adjustments.

On other occasions, MNEs' organisational coherence involves more subjective factors rooted in their culture, self-image and history.

One case in point relates to the lessons that a company has drawn from its own history, whether its initial experiences in its home market or else its internationalisation trajectory (how fast it grew, its risk attitudes and confidence in its ability to run foreign subsidiaries). Another variable is managers' adaptability, meaning their capacity for coping in different kinds of organisations as well as their willingness to cede part of their power and authority if need be..

These latter variables speak to the latent human forces at work in MNEs like any business or social entity. It is one thing to explicitly publicise departmental boundaries and hierarchical relationships – it is another to analyse the fit with the people actually working at the company. Individuals are not robots. They will always bring their personal mindsets and affinities to the workplace. Conflict is inevitable and can be especially hard to manage in an international environment where employee values and notions of self-interest (see Chapter 4) are particularly divergent. Hence the enormous efforts most MNEs make to maximise employees' adherence to their corporate culture (see Chapter 5) – an effort requiring sociological understanding of how organisational roles interact.

Sociology of (multinational) organisations

The overriding principles driving organisational decision-making often reflect international business studies' linkage of theoretical and practical concerns.

- Centralisation
  This refers to the extent to which an MNE's head office shares power with subsidiaries. Professionals will have a natural interest in monopolising knowledge (hence power) but quickly learn that keeping colleagues out of the loop can de-motivate them and make them perform less well. This raises a broader question whether employees are satisfied with the particular role they have been assigned within the MNE – and whether they therefore accept the amount of power their superiors have captured or require that more be shared.
- Hierarchy
  This principle is rooted in the recognition of authority. MNE reporting lines are often confusing. Where workers in a domestic company usually work near their boss and are therefore clear about expectations, MNE employees often have two bosses: the local country manager; and the person in charge of their product or

functional area. Things can get complicated when the latter works in another time zone – especially if the two bosses have different business philosophies (regarding, for instance, pricing, product adaptation, or customer segmentation).

- Specialisation

  This is one solution to the confusion over people's multiple roles within an MNE. Defining narrow missions is not always possible, however, especially in SMEs where, by definition, fewer people are work, meaning that each has several roles to fulfil. Large MNEs do have the advantage of being able to specialise staff so that everyone gains greater expertise in a particular area of competency. The problem is that this can create a silo mentality and tunnel vision hampering employees' willingness to share useful knowledge outside of their own department.

- Coordination

  The more specialised employees' missions are within an organisation, the harder it is to coordinate them. A good way to visualise this is by imagining that each employee has a "territory" to manage. This can be defined along functional lines (one stage in the value chain) but also in terms of products or geography. The company needs to ensure that all these territories fit together in a way that avoids duplication while maximising performance.

  Territorial conflicts are frequent in MNEs, often because one team has the ambition of taking over another's business. It may be in the company's interest for both teams to coordinate. But if they have separate bonus pools – as is frequently the case in fragmented multinational organisations - they are likely to see things differently.

- Control

  Companies spend considerable resources on controlling performance. In widely dispersed MNEs where managers work far from their teams, getting feedback can be difficult, however. Visits to foreign colleagues are often advisable in this case, but they are expensive and generally only occur sporadically. Hence the global (or at least regional) reporting systems that MNEs develop to compensate for this deficiency. It remains that information transmitted over long distances does not always paint a full picture of what is happening in far off subsidiaries. Country managers have a vested interest in protecting their teams from head office interference and may not communicate all relevant facts. And head office executives suffering from information overload may not have the time to cope with anything more than short and necessarily incomplete reports. One constant in international business today is that people are incredibly busy. The ensuing need for abbreviated communications undermines managers' overall control, however.

Bibliography

Bartlett, C. and Ghoshal, S. (1989), *Managing across Borders: The Transnational Solution*, Harvard Business School Press.

Buckley, P. (2010), "Stephen Hymer: Three Phases, One Approach?", in *Foreign Direct Investment: China and the World Economy*, Palgrave Macmillan.

Levitt, T. (1983), "The Globalization of Markets", *Harvard Business Review*, https://hbr.org/1983/05/the-globalization-of-markets

UNCTAD (update continuously), *Transnationality Index*, http://unctad.org/en/Pages/DIAE/World Investment Report/Largest-TNCs.aspx

World Bank (update annually), *Doing Business*, https://www.doingbusiness.org

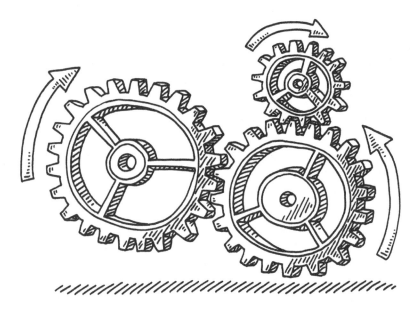

On the road again.

8 International upstream operations

Essential summary

One of international managers' most crucial value chain decisions is the width of the product range their company should offer. At one extreme, MNEs can opt for a standardised high-volume production of a narrow range of goods. At the other, they can emphasise adaptation and offer a wide range of items capable of pleasing a diverse international clientele. Generally speaking, manufacturing companies 'prefer the former, which enables economies of scale helping them achieve their operational goal of making goods cheaply and efficiently. Downstream specialists tend to support a wider and more customised product range facilitating sales into different markets. These contradictory interests cause tension within MNE value chains and explains why upstream and downstream interests (Chapter 9) are indissociable.

Knowledge as the first step in production

Business performance starts with a company's ability to transform knowledge into processes and products. Clearly, knowledge management (KM) is important across the value chain. Even so, many top MNEs have built their success on production advantages specifically by transforming intangible bundles of knowledge into new products or services.

International KM can be apprehended at both the macro (national) level and in terms of MNEs' research and development (R&D) efforts. Regarding the former, an economy's overall level of technological advancement largely depends on the quantum of "knowledge spillovers" between companies, universities, research centres and government, conceptualised altogether by French economists Robert Boyer and Michel Freyssenet as the "national innovation system". Markets vary widely in terms of "R&D intensity", or the percentage of GDP spent on R&D. Much international business is driven by MNEs' desire to gain knowledge by entering environments where they can nurture and/or access knowledge – and by national governments' desire to attract MNEs capable of enhancing local knowledge.

From a corporate perspective, one of R&D's main characteristics is its costliness. There is rarely any certainty that a product innovation will sell well enough globally to justify initial R&D outlays, which are enormous in certain sectors. Many MNEs spend so much on R&D that they cannot afford the commercial networks needed to distribute their innovations worldwide – even though global sales are the only hope of recouping the substantial upfront investment. Strategic alliances often involve rival MNEs forced into co-operation due to the cost of R&D. This applies particularly to SMEs.

Since knowledge is key to international competitiveness, MNEs strive to protect intellectual property rights, often through exclusivity arrangements. A distinction is commonly made between whether a particular type of knowledge constitutes a public good or not. Confidentiality is difficult to maintain when a company internationalises and MNEs may choose to only transfer less strategic categories of knowledge, relating for instance to management practices instead of product characteristics.

A final distinction can be made between "push R&D", where MNEs force innovations on the market, and "pull R&D", where the company is responding to market signals. Push R&D is often concentrated on a single site, usually global headquarters, to maximise confidentiality and reduce overheads. This means, however, that researchers are working at a distance from the various markets that their new product will affect. They might therefore be tempted to impose a single global standard instead of catering to different market preferences. Pull MNEs, on the other hand, tend to run multiple R&D centres to keep researchers in contact with the customers affected by their innovations – a phenomenon further explored in Chapter 11's analysis of international talent management trends. Of course, duplicating operations in multiple centres is costly.

It is impossible to overstate the importance of knowledge management as an international production factor. Decisions taken at the early stages of a value chain will have crucial knock-on effects as products or services evolve into their final shape. Managers must always consider the ripple effects of the upstream decisions they take.

Global supply chain management

Supply chain management (SCM) refers to all operations sourcing, producing, transporting, assembling and finalising a product or service. Global SCM is when firms are in a position to purchase, deliver or take delivery of raw materials, components and modules anywhere in the world.

The first dividing line in global SCM (see Figure 8.1) is whether an MNE sources raw materials and components from an external supplier

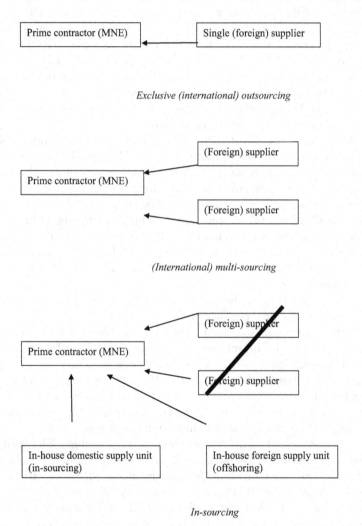

Figure 8.1 International supply chain systems.

or from a foreign unit that it owns. The latter solution, involving vertically integrated MNEs' "offshoring" configuration, raises a number of logistics and production location issues. The former refers to international "outsourcing", a leading driver of international business today.

International outsourcing

There are several explanations for the recent rise in outsourcing. With the spread of the shareholder value paradigm that American CEO Jack Welch first conceptualised in the 1980s, MNEs began prioritising financial performance indicators like return on equity (ROE) over objectives like market share. One way to increase ROE is by "shrinking the balance sheet". This is because there are fewer assets to finance if some production functions are no longer run in-house. It is also easier and cheaper during periods of economic downturn to re-negotiate supplier contracts than to shut down factories.

MNEs today are less daunted by the kinds of coordination problems that arise when foreign suppliers enter their production process. First, companies applying a "multi-sourcing" approach can diversify their supplier shortlist and ensure continued competition for orders. A similar advantage is attained when MNEs centralise global procurement for all subsidiaries, thereby enabling bulk purchasing. Otherwise, inter-firm communications have been greatly enhanced in recent years by Electronic Data Interchanges (EDI) and other online applications optimising the inter-firm flow of goods. As a result, some of the world's best-known MNEs (including Nike but also to some extent Dell and Ikea) are referred to as "hollow firms" that only manufacture a small percentage of the final products they sell.

With simpler goods, outsourcing often sees companies leveraging suppliers' own cost advantages and/or economies of scale. For more complex goods, there is the added benefit of being able to access suppliers' technological know-how. In both cases, by outsourcing non-essential functions, firms free themselves up to focus on what strategy researchers C.K. Prahalad and Gary Hamel have famously referred to as the "core competencies" where they can be most productive.

Of course, international outsourcing has shortcomings. The "prime contractor" becomes dependent on external suppliers, losing the ability to produce its own inputs and the specialist knowledge associated with this – a vulnerability that became particularly apparent following the eruption of the COVID-19 pandemic. This can be dangerous when adverse currency or raw material price movements increase component prices. The same applies when an MNE's brand reputation suffers as a result of suppliers' unethical labour or environmental practices.

Lastly, outsourcing sometimes undercuts the "lean production" principles that many MNEs apply today, one of which highlights the need to reduce inventory costs by having inputs delivered "just-in-time". It can be risky for a company to source materials from distant suppliers since longer lead times increase the likelihood of late deliveries upsetting production schedules.

Solutions do exist for these distance-related problems, however. Radio frequency identification technology (RFID) enabling real-time tracking and inventory management helps contractors forecast deliveries and manage inventories more accurately. Otherwise, some MNEs build "supplier parks" adjacent to their overseas assembly plants to shorten supply lines. Lastly, "near-shoring" has seen many prime contractors opting for suppliers who may not be the cheapest but whose proximity to the MNE's assembly units reduces supplies' time in transit.

Where the cost of remedying international outsourcing's shortcomings outweighs its advantages, MNEs may be tempted to bring back in-house ("in-source") supply functions that were previously externalised. Outsourcing's benefits are constantly weighed against its disadvantages.

Types of supply relationships

International supplier relationships differentiate between the short-term, so-called American model; the longer-term, so-called Asian model; and a hybrid of the two.

In the short-term model, subcontractors bid (for instance, via online auction platforms) whenever a contractor replenishes stocks. This puts them at constant risk of losing business if they slip on quality and/or price. There is little room for loyalty or joint planning in such relationships, but they do force suppliers to stay competitive.

Longer-term supply models focus on collaboration. Encapsulated in Japanese *keiretsus*, Korean *chaebols* and Chinese *guanxi* networks, these are prime examples of business being embedded in cultural contexts. In a *keiretsu*, for instance, the prime contractor lends its name to a network of companies that collaborate on all the upstream operations needed to bring a good to market. Firms typically take an equity stake in one another and plan investments, R&D and products together. This is a comfortable arrangement based on stable contracts that are usually renewed without non-*keiretsu* members being allowed to compete. Even in cases of "follow sourcing" where subcontractors build factories abroad to service prime contractors' own overseas operations, *keiretsu* suppliers can still count on winning most contracts. Predictability of this kind is priceless since it helps suppliers' industrial planners to size plant capacities correctly – an advantage translating ultimately into lower costs that can be shared across the value chain. Having said that, the lack of competition means the prime contractor is beholden to the decisions made by its long-term (hence potentially very complacent) supplier.

A number of MNEs have moved over the years to create a compromise model, developing shortlists of suppliers who remain autonomous but receive financial, technological or personnel support. Theorised by Professor Alan Rugman as a "flagship firm" model, the benefits for the prime contractor is that it can count on reliable supplies and faces a lesser risk that suppliers will take advantage of tight conditions to raise prices. It can also internationalise more quickly since there is no need to build its own manufacturing facilities.

Suppliers also benefit from early industrial collaboration in the form of "concurrent engineering" by sharing the prime contractor's technological expertise. This ensures "fractal" coherence between the modules that production partners are making. Suppliers can also piggyback their customer's ability to buy raw materials in bulk, thus cheaply. Above all, they enjoy greater stability, with guaranteed sales volumes allowing them to size production capacities more accurately.

However, suppliers tied into such arrangements incur extra costs, if only because they are still building expensive, capital-intensive manufacturing units. Indeed, outsourcing sometimes sees prime contractors passing onto their suppliers the performance pressures that they themselves face. Like most aspects of international business, supply chain management is best analysed in light of managers' strategic paradigms – epitomised in this area by what the *Harvard Busines Review* has called the Triple-A supply chain model emphasising agility, alignment and adaptability.

International production

MNEs can only satisfy international demands for a timely delivery of different goods to different locations if they have an efficient manufacturing and logistics network. Ideas about the best way of devising such networks vary, however. Hence the value of starting a study of international production by scrutinising the different industrial models that MNEs have implemented over the years.

Industrial models

The mass production system that Henry Ford first applied around a century ago offered standardisation and efficiency advantages. By maximising economies of scale, Ford's system cut costs, enabling lower retail prices hence higher sales. It is the seminal international production system.

As powerful as Fordism was, however, it had several flaws, starting with the emphasis on uniformity. This may be acceptable in a new product's early stages but as a market matures and/or internationalises, consumers may want more diversity. That is problematic for Fordist manufacturers. Offering a wide product range is expensive, if only because of the time lost switching between different factory assembly lines. Shorter production runs also diminish economies of scale.

To solve this problem while still reaping the benefits of mass production, Ford's great rival at General Motors during the 1920s, Alfred Sloan, came up with the idea of "deferred differentiation" (or "postponement") where manufacturers still achieve economies of scale by making invisible sub-assemblies using the same components, even as they give consumers a sense of variety by differentiating the visible parts bolted onto products during final assembly (see Figure 8.2). The strength of this approach – combining scale with diversity – explains

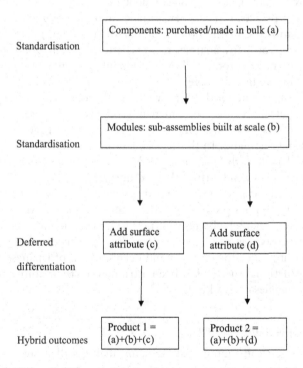

Figure 8.2 Deferred differentiation combining productive standardisation with adaptation.

its lasting popularity for international business practitioners. Having said that, Sloan's system also had its imperfections, requiring manufacturers to carry large hence expensive inventories of parts and depending excessively on the accuracy of factory managers' ex ante volume predictions.

It was largely because of these shortcomings that a new industrial model, called the "Toyota Production System", became dominant in the 1970s. The idea here is that volume manufacturing can coincide with product flexibility as long as waste is minimised through better management of factory flows ("throughput").

This can be achieved in several ways. First, staff members adopt a bottom-up, *kaizen* (continuous improvement) attitude, the idea being that the people actually responsible for production operations are best placed to know how to increase efficiency. Employees meet regularly in "quality circles" to discuss process improvements. In a world characterised by increasingly knowledgeable consumers, quality has become a factor in all industrial models, but none more so than Toyotaism, dominated by a Total Quality Management (TQM) philosophy targeting zero output defects. Quality performance and monitoring, often based on International Organisation for Standardisation (ISO) principles, is a leading topic in many analyses of international production, but it can also be a marketing tool, with MNEs brandishing their ISO certification to improve brand image.

The second noteworthy aspect of the Toyota Production System is its revolutionary inventory management process. Here, the prime contractor asks subcontractors to replenish stocks at a rate defined by real customer demand. In this *kanban* (automatic signalling) approach, supply orders at each level of the value chain are pulled by the next level downstream, and ultimately by orders from end users. The system contrasts with one where replenishment is pushed by factory schedules, which are poor predictors of flows in firms serving volatile hence opaque global markets. By preventing surplus production, *kanban* keeps inventory costs down. Conversely, in those instances where supplies run short, it reduces bottlenecks and delays. Much of Japanese companies' international success has been attributed to their ability to apply "lean" principles of this kind.

Logistics and plant location

Clearly, a vertically integrated company making all its own components faces different pressures than one that outsources everything and whose only production activity involves assembling finished products or simply branding ones built by other companies. For many MNEs, the reality lies between these two extremes – they run some strategic operations in-house and outsource the rest. The ability to link these flows via logistics is therefore crucial.

Logistics matter at all supply chain levels, from initial inputs to product recycling ("reverse logistics"). Global competition means that deliveries of raw materials, components and finished products must be quicker and more flexible than ever. This puts enormous pressure on logistics professionals. Sometimes the pressure come from the downstream: retailers requiring suppliers to replenish geographically distant outlets all at once; or online shoppers forcing retailers to compete on delivery performance. On other occasions, the pressure is on the production-side, relating to the need to replenish globally dispersed assembly sites or prevent inventory accumulating in the form of finished products, where it is most expensive. It is only through top logistics performance that international manufacturers can cope.

Most MNEs are incapable of this without help, however. Logistics requires not only physical capabilities but also specific knowledge about geography and infrastructure as well as documentary and regulatory requirements, customs administration and banking practices. Sometimes a company will take responsibility for a shipment on a cost, insurance and freight (CIF) basis. On other occasions, it leaves these tasks to its counterpart and simply makes or takes delivery of the goods on a free on board (FOB) basis. This is an important distinction, not only because it reflects the MNE's confidence in its ability to organise logistics but because each of these "Incoterms" implies different legal rights and obligations. Documents like "bills of lading" have evolved to convey information about the nature of goods in transit, carriage details and above all transfer of ownership procedures. Specialist customs house brokers and freight forwarders "clear" goods through customs on MNEs' account, paying duties where required and organising further transportation from the point of arrival to final destination. Bank "trade finance" departments offer an array of financial instruments, including "letters of credit" reassuring sellers that they will be paid once buyers or their agents take ownership of the goods. Logistics in its broadest sense covers a very wide range of trade operations that are just as important as the physical movement of goods. International business would be impossible without the armies of specialist third party logistics providers performing this function.

Logistics also affect MNEs' production location decisions in various ways. One is by enabling "centralised inventories" with MNEs storing global stocks of semi-finished and finished products in just a few key regional distribution centres (often untaxed free trade zones). This has the advantage of reducing overheads but also increases the distance between an MNE's storage facilities and consumer markets, potentially slowing delivery times. To compensate, many companies offer customers joint information systems similar to the ones they operate with suppliers. Such information-sharing also constitutes a logistics solution.

Analogous to centralised inventories are the "focused factories" that some MNEs build to specialise each of their productive units in a given activity, thereby increasing plant-level economies of scale. Of course, reducing the number of production locations in this way also causes longer product lead times while complicating packaging and communications, something that can be problematic when an MNE wants to service a global customer's large consolidated order for goods manufactured in different focused factories worldwide. In this case, the rationale for the MNE's plant location decisions must be juggled against its logistics constraints.

All in all, production location tends to be determined by proximity to resources, knowledge spillover possibilities, host government attitudes and most importantly the size and importance of the market(s) that a factory is meant to service. Some plants only serve the countries or regions where they are located. Others ship output globally, either to sister MNE units or directly to customers. A key distinction is between plants that merely assemble modules produced elsewhere, and others that manufacture generic goods. The former are cheaper and less capital-intensive, hence easier to disperse. This differs from big manufacturing plants, which by their very nature cost more and are therefore less likely to be replicated. The terms "manufacturing" or "production" refer to overlapping but different activities and should not be viewed as synonymous. Precise use of terminology is another crucial skill for international business practitioners.

Bibliography

Basu, R. and Wright, J. N. (2016), *Managing Global Supply Chains*, Routledge (2nd edition).

De Marchi, V. et al. (eds) (2018), *Local Clusters in Global Value Chains*, Routledge.

Edwards, R. and Howell, A, (1998), "Multinational Corporation Strategy: Implications for Research and Development", *R & D Enterprise: Asia Pacific*, Volume 1, No. 5–6, pp. 3–10.

Marti, K. et al. (August 2014), "The Importance of Logistics Performance Index in International Trade", *Applied Economics*, Volume 46, No. 24, pp. 2982–2992.

Miltenburg, J. (2005), *Manufacturing Strategy*, Routledge (2nd edition).

"Let's give them a choice".

9 International downstream operations

Essential summary

When entering a foreign market, MNEs face a classic international business dilemma: whether they should adapt their product or service to local consumers' needs or opt for standardisation. Weighing each approach's trade-offs and analysing global, regional and local demographic trends can help international marketers to make the right decisions. Often, a balanced approach needs to be carefully crafted to ensure the firm's success overseas.

There is little doubt that people, events, products, and places worldwide have become infinitely more connected in recent decades. Global customers may order a Big Mac and a Coke in most countries whilst sharing photos on Instagram with friends located in multiple locations and using an Uber taxi service to reach their next meeting. From this perspective, it seems that humans share many of the same needs, tastes and habits worldwide. MNEs' complex response to consumers' sense of proximity and behavioural convergence may result in the decision to adapt to local markets and cultures. McDonald's menu, for instance, includes Rice Burgers in Hong Kong and My Poutine in Canada; Coca Cola develops different flavours of Coke to appeal to the tastes of local customers. Indeed, the perception that the world has become uniform and homogeneous can be challenged by significant variations in the extent to which otherwise successful MNEs have been willing to adapt their products and services. When expanding overseas, MNEs make important decisions regarding their marketing strategies. Although marketing techniques may be similar to those used in domestic markets, they are likely to be performed differently in foreign markets.

This chapter explores key factors for analysing international marketing and deciding whether to standardise or adapt a firm's product/service to its local target market. The marketing mix strategy is then discussed from an international business perspective.

Analysing a foreign market

Marketing research includes the collection and analysis of data, which combine to help marketers make better decisions when expanding overseas. There are three kinds of markets worth considering when developing a product/service and expanding internationally: consumer, industrial and governmental. Each market can then be segmented into smaller categories to delineate the market potential, sales potential and level of adaptation/standardisation required.

International market analysis

The foundation of any internationalisation strategy is market research. Surveying international demographics is a determinant marketing activity, supporting managers' decision-making process when considering overseas expansion. Factors in international market analysis include the potential host country's population, per capita GDP, demographic composition and societal or cultural norms.

The key trend at this level is the sheer rise in the global population, as well as the increasing solvency of previously impoverished households in the world's emerging Global South economies (see Chapter 12). In and of itself, this trend suggests that global demand for goods and services is likely to increase during the 21st century. The United Nations has forecast, for instance, that the current world population of 7.6 billion is likely to reach 8.6 billion in 2030, 9.8 billion in 2050, and 11.2 billion in 2100. Moreover, there are likely to be some changes in the current global rankings of countries by population size. China (with 1.4 billion inhabitants) and India (1.3 billion inhabitants) are presently the world's two most populous countries, comprising, respectively, 19% and 18% of total world population. India's population is expected to surpass that of China by around 2025, however, with Nigeria – currently the 7th most populated county, – expected to surpass the US by 2050.

Another key aspect is population ageing, combined with a dramatic decrease in fertility rates worldwide. According to the United Nations, the number of persons aged 60 or above is expected to more than double by 2050 and more than triple by 2100. In Europe, 25% of the population is already aged 60 years or over, a number expected to reach 35% in 2050. These trends have a direct effect on the future prospects of certain international markets, exemplified in the ageing countries by a growing demand for healthcare and pharmaceuticals, hence bio-technology. In other nations characterised by a rapidly rising population of young households, on the other hand, the most promising sectors include food and household durables. MNEs will examine global demographic trends of this kind in order to define their next internationalisation move.

Another frequently used analytic is a prospective host country's Gross Domestic Product (GDP) , which measures the total annual value of the goods and services traded in an economy – hence, indirectly, income and, carrying on from that, purchasing power. Note that these numbers are often usefully represented on a per capita basis, where national totals are divided by the population to get the average per person. According to the International Monetary Fund (IMF)'s 2019 estimates, the three economic territories (sovereign and non-sovereign entities) with the highest GDP per capita were Qatar ($132,886), Macau ($114,363), and Luxembourg ($108,951). By contrast, many other nations, some located on the African continent, have a GDP per capita of less than $5,000, the lowest being Burundi ($727). These statistics will vary over time but do offer an indication of different international markets' current sales potential.

In the end, MNEs conduct international market research analysis with a view towards developing factual underpinnings for the expansion strategies they have set themselves. Having said that, MNEs are not always willing to pay independent consultants for these market reports, which can be very expensive. Instead, they will often rely on the local knowledge of managers and marketers. This may lead to damaging and costly mistakes if a product, distribution or marketing campaign turns out to be inadequate for a particular target market. In the end, the role that an international manager plays in an MNE's downstream decision-making – hence, where s/he works in its structure (see Chapter 7) – will be crucial to the formulation and/or identification of a successful international marketing effort.

Market Intelligence Systems and big data analytics

The aphorism "knowledge is power" applies well to marketing activities in an international business environment. MNEs increasingly develop Market Intelligence Systems (MIS) encompassing the systematic collection and processing of primary and secondary data from all relevant sources in order to develop an in-depth understanding of the changing trends in the marketing environment and support critical decisions in the internationalisation of a company. This may involve, for instance, interviews, focus groups and mail surveys, all of which will be combined with a compilation of longitudinal data about the foreign country in which an MNE intends to operate.

There are two types of data at this level: secondary (composed of existing internal reports, external publications and databases); and primary (relating to quantitative and qualitative studies undertaken by the company as well as information gathered in business meetings with partners and during trade shows). Once an MNE has entered a foreign market, big data analytics may also provide valuable insights into local consumer behaviour, which can be used to increase sales and improve Customer Relationship Management (CRM) systems. Big data analytics for marketing purposes represents a booming sector driven by the growing adoption of technology across the globe. Chapter 11 looks at this phenomenon in greater detail, including the implications for international business careers.

International marketing framework

MNEs willing to market overseas have four options to consider. They can sell the same domestic product overseas (standardisation);they can adapt their product to the different countries and regions where they operate (adaptation); existing products/services can be extended or re-developed to meet the specific needs and regulations in a country or region (glocalisation); and/or the product variations present in different countries can be integrated and used as a basis for developing a brand that will then be sold into many if not most overseas markets (global branding). Note that these strategies are not necessarily mutually exclusive, in the sense that some MNEs may apply certain approaches in one market and a different one elsewhere. Conversely, other MNEs may follow the same downstream strategy in all of the markets where they operate worldwide. As with other kinds of strategic choices, it is this diversity that makes MNEs' international marketing calculations so interesting to explore.

Standardisation vs adaptation

One of the most impactful decisions that a company must make when entering a foreign market is related to the degree of similarity between their international marketing strategy and the domestic one. All aspects of international marketing strategy are concerned with this daunting decision whether product, promotion, distribution, and pricing (see "International marketing mix"). Neither is perfect under all circumstances, however, meaning that decisions in this area inevitably involve trade-offs.

Standardisation

When MNEs adopt a standardisation approach, their international marketing strategy is similar to the one implemented domestically. Examples here might include computer and other electronics companies whose key factor of success is technical, and who therefore only make minimal changes to their products when seeking to penetrate a foreign market. The main advantages of this approach are its low cost, relative facility, and, above all, the economies of scale it permits. Existing corporate functions (e.g. research & development) can be replicated without the additional expense of developing a new market entry approach. Another advantage is that existing marketing operations (e.g. advertising, promotion, etc.) can be implemented quickly in overseas markets.

Adaptation

By contrast, the adaptation approach means that international marketing strategies used in foreign markets are different from those deployed in the company's home market. Frequent examples of this approach are found in the food sector, possibly due to the fact that food preferences are deeply entrenched in societies worldwide – with numerous cases of MNEs attempting to introduce a new foodstuff to a foreign market and failing there, only to return a few years later with a successfully adapted problem. The problem is that adaptation typically requires higher initial costs than does standardisation, because of the need to open up new production lines but also due to the need to staff the downstream function with staff well-versed in the particularities of the local market. These disadvantages then need to be judged against the potential higher sales in the target foreign market as the MNE accounts for the specific tastes and needs of local customers.

Striking the right balance

Glocalisation

MNEs often find a compromise between adaptation and standardisation, called glocalisation. This strategy involves standardising when possible and adapting when necessary to meet the needs of consumers in a foreign market. For many companies this is downstream equivalent of the upstream "deferred differentiation" strategy referred to in Chapter 8 – and also tantamount to the compromise "transactional" strategy (see Chapter 7) that numerous MNEs apply in a bid to combine the advantages of both the global and the local approaches – being, as a subset of the standardisation-adaptation debate, one of the key decisions that any international business practitioner will have to make.

Glocalisation as an international downstream consideration includes the debate about which particular aspects of a product or service's marketing mixed should be globalised or localised. This can be the product itself and/or its pricing and/or its advertising. The first thing to note at this level is the possibility of standardising or else adapting certain aspects of an item in some countries but different ones in other countries. The issue then becomes who makes the decisions at this level, raising questions as to the location within the MNE where power has been vested – and to the cultural and other worldviews of the individuals exercising this power. The normal balance sees people empowered at the local subsidiary level emphasising the particularities of the market where they find themselves but displaying less acumen about global downstream strategies – with headquarters marketing managers possessing the opposite strengths and weaknesses.

Global branding and the associated risks

A combination of product and market factors may explain why MNEs opt for standardisation or adaptation. The BrandZ Top Global Brands list provides some insights into which types of products/services seem to require minimal adaptation yet benefit from maximum recognition and visibility at a global level. In recent years, companies such as Amazon, Apple, Google, Microsoft and Visa – but also Chinese brands such as Alibaba (retail) and Tencent (technology) – have come at the top of the list. The lesson that can be derived from this is that technology – along with a few luxury brands (such as Louis Vuitton and Chanel) – transfers most easily across borders, The potential explanation for the relative ease with which these kinds of products travel is that they are modern and therefore less deeply embedded in the cultures and preferences that societies developed separately back in the days when there was less global interconnection than is the case today.

Global branding strategies do have a notable downside, however, being the prevalence of counterfeits that damage the reputation and sales of the products affected. Counterfeits appear among all types of equipment/products, from defence equipment to prescription drugs and luxury goods (e.g. watches, bags, perfume). The value of the global market for counterfeits is enormous, accounting according to certain studies to tens of billions of dollars annually for luxury brands alone – with the total global value of fake merchandise being counted in the trillions. Counterfeiting is a long-standing and ever-growing issue in global trade. Government and MNEs are concerned by the adverse impact of such illicit activities on businesses and society – in part because counterfeiting can also threaten consumers (e.g. fake medicine), not to mention companies' reputation. Despite the use of new technology, legal action and lobbying, MNEs often struggle to contain this problem, particularly in some of the emerging economies where future international market growth seems most promising.

Product Life Cycle

The Product Life Cycle (PLC) is a useful concept for managing products' market introduction and is particularly relevant to international marketers deciding when to modify their cross-border strategies. PLC represents the sales and profits of a new product over its lifetime in one specific market (Figure 9.1). Its value as a construct in international business lies in the way any one product can be at a different stage of its PLC in one country as opposed to another.

Based on PLC reasoning, international marketers are constantly looking for foreign markets – preferably mass ones – where their products may be in a growth stage, therefore justifying initial investment as the item hits its prime. By contrast, because product prices decline

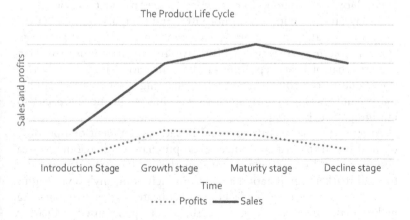

Figure 9.1 The Product Life Cycle.

during a market's maturity phase (due to the rise of local and/or global competition), this is often taken as a signal that it is time to abandon it. Indeed, where the maturing market is a company's home country, this is often the initial impetus for it to go abroad, i.e. become an MNE, in the hope of finding a foreign market where their product can be more attractive to and relevant for local consumers. Examples include telephone companies taking stocks of outdated models and selling them in less affluent markets where the lower price is a more important sales argument that having the absolutely latest technology. Managing different PLCs in different national markets is a key aspect of most MNEs' international downstream decision-making.

International marketing mix

The four underlying components of the marketing mix are commonly called the 4 Ps: Product, Place, Price, and Promotion. MNEs use the same tools and techniques to reach customers domestically and internationally, but tend to apply them differently in each case.

Product

Products are merchandised goods or services. As discussed, firms operating at an international level are concerned with the level of standardisation or adaptation of their offerings in different markets. Theodore Levitt opined, in his seminal article *"The Globalisation of Markets"* (1983), that standardisation is a good marketing strategy for products such as watches or Hollywood movies when exploiting advantages of scales. However, attempts to market unchanged products/services overseas may fall flat, with the ethnocentric and even arrogant belief that "one size fits all" being a prime factor in some of the costly international marketing errors that MNEs have historically committed. Having said that, it bears repeating product adaptation is easier said than done, due to the cost incurred when adapting a product to a foreign market and because many companies have limited financial capacity for engaging in such changes.

Another alternative can be found in the development of a portfolio of local brands to match the needs and purchasing behaviours of local customers. In this case, international marketers pay particular attention to local market segmentation and ignore their company's own origins. Of course, the ideal at this level is to delineate market segments (e.g. male/female, urban/rural, age, etc.) that can be generalised in a variety of foreign markets.

Overall, many customers worldwide share similar purchasing habits, interests, needs and preferences. But many others do not. As a rule of thumb, products embedded in culture, such as food, education, and cosmetics, typically require more adaptation than computers, tennis rackets, and chemical processes. Some of these changes will be required to match host country market standards (regulations, physical realities). Others will reflect the MNE's own appraisal of the situation. It is in this latter area that the greatest international business successes but also failures are experienced.

Place

Place commonly refers to the location where a product is sold, either physically or digitally. In international marketing, distribution channels refer to the different ways in which a firm may bring their product to customers in foreign markets. This is a key decision, closely related to the mode of entry selected by a firm entering a foreign market, including exporting, licencing/franchising, turnkey projects, wholly owned subsidiaries, joint ventures, and mergers and acquisitions (see Chapter 6). Also, international marketers must consider local infrastructure, internet penetration and online channels to adjust their strategy without undermining traditional distribution network (e.g. "bricks and mortar").

Price

Price refers to the expense that customers are inclined to pay for a product or service. Undeniably, firms incur additional costs when going international, in terms of either logistics (when the market entry mode involves exports) or FDI. Consequently, goods are often a more expensive overseas than at home. To justify these higher prices, international marketers may position goods to align them with stereotypes about and attitudes towards equivalent foreign products in the host country. Yet concerns can still arise if consumers in one country become aware that a product being sold to them as top-of-the-line is sold elsewhere as midrange or even a basic commodity.

A variety of factors affect the suitability of international pricing choices. One is foreign exchange (see Chapter 10), with problems arising if the currency in which sales are made falls compared to the currency in which production costs are incurred. Another is government regulations. In some countries, minimum and maximum prices to customers are imposed on international firms. Governments may also prohibit dumping (see Chapter 3), which is widely considered an unfair competitive practice (and one that is the source of a number trade wars currently being waged between countries like the USA and China).

Otherwise, price elasticity is also a key factor in international marketing, being the relationship between price changes and demand. A leading task for many international marketing managers is estimating overseas customers' familiarity with their products and reckon how demand for their products will vary as incomes evolve (a particularly important issue in Global South countries undergoing rapid development). A frequent problem here is the generally tendency towards over-pricing, with managers assuming that foreign consumers are more interested in their products than they really are. Wrong decisions made in this area often reflect over-confidence, pride, or even arrogance of some decision-makers in MNEs' global headquarters. In marketing as in other areas of international business, personal psychology can be just as important as business strategy.

Promotion

Promotion encompasses all communication delivered by a firm to reach potential customers. It includes advertising, TV, radio, social media, direct mail, billboards, direct marketing (personal selling) and public relations. International marketers also face a standardisation vs adaptation dilemma here in terms of the messages they choose to send to a global and/or local audience. On the one hand, standardisation enables the transmission of a constant message supporting global branding strategy while limiting advertising agency costs. However, numerous MNEs have learned the hard way that advertising is highly embedded in the local culture, customs and language. Semiotics, the study of signs, symbols and their meaning in a particular context, may prove essential for international marketers. There are myriad examples of a mistranslation of brands or products creating confusion and rejection among local customers. The end result is that a local approach to advertising is often necessary when entering foreign markets, despite the considerable expense to MNEs.

It remains that international advertising is huge business, with global spending exceeding half a trillion dollars by the start of the 2020s, up more than 40% from the decade before. With such large sums to play, it becomes an immensely strategic issue for MNEs to decide who within their organisation is responsible for designing advertising campaigns and if the money saved on showing the same advertisement in different countries compensates for the risk of its being less effective with a particular target market. At this level like so many others in international business, the key is the arbitrage that the MNE makes between its internal interests and external stakeholders' preference for diversity.

Bibliography

Crawford, R. (ed.) et al (2017). Global Advertising Practice in a Borderless World, Routledge

Fontana R., Girod S. J. G., & Králik M., (24/05/2019) "How Luxury Brands Can Beat Counterfeiters", *Harvard Business Review*, available at https://hbr.org/2019/05/how-luxury-brands-can-beat-counterfeiters, last accessed: 04/03/2020

Klein, N. (1999), *No Logo*, Picador.

Levitt, T. (1983), The Globalization of Markets, *Harvard Business Review*.

Money isn't funny

10 Multinational finance

Essential summary

The two main topics in multinational finance are foreign exchange (FX) and treasury. In terms of the former, MNEs monitor their positions at all times to avoid the kinds of adverse currency movements that can wipe out profits. Tracking a group's innumerable positions is extremely difficult, however, explaining why most MNEs spend large sums on information systems centralising currency data. As for MNEs' treasury operations, the key here is their ability to access capital for both short and long-term purposes. When times are tough, acquiring finance can be crucial to a company's expansion and even survival. Like labour or materials, funding is a key input in an MNE's production process.

Foreign exchange

The only MNEs that avoid direct foreign exchange (FX) risk are those who operate entirely in their home currency. And even so, they still face indirect risk because of the way currency movements affect their international rivals' competitiveness.

For the vast majority of MNEs, currency risk is a permanent phenomenon. The main questions then become how this risk manifests itself; where it originates; and what might be done about it.

The concept of exposure

By definition, the vast majority of MNEs engage in FX simply because they incur costs and/or generate revenues in multi-currency environments as a matter of course. On top of this, there are certain commodities like oil or rubber (or complex goods like aeroplanes) where the US dollar is globally recognised as the standard currency of transaction. This automatically creates FX exposures for non-dollar-based companies trading in these sectors.

In general, an MNE is exposed to FX risk under the following conditions:

- Its assets and/or liabilities are denominated in several currencies.
- A gap exists between its assets and liabilities in any one currency.
- Prices vary for the currencies in question – reflecting in turn whether a currency is pegged to a fixed rate set by the government or (as has overwhelmingly become the case since the 1970s and the end of the gold standard) if its price floats and reflects continuous trading between market participants.

Where a firm has more assets than liabilities in a given currency (a "long" position), the risk is that the currency falls in value before the assets can be sold. Where a firm has more liabilities than assets in a given currency (a "short" position), the risk is that it rises in value before the liabilities can be acquired. Thus, regardless of a firm's currency of origin, it is exposed to FX price variations if its various positions are not equal to zero at all times.

Sources of FX exposure

"Transactional" exposures are incurred through value chain activities. These are MNEs' main FX risks and can occur regularly or sporadically.

- *Commercial risk* arises when an MNEs is paid in foreign currency, increasing its long exposure.
- *Operational risk* occurs when it makes payments in a foreign currency, increasing its short exposure.

Most MNEs manage the FX exposures that their various international subsidiaries accumulate on a net basis. This means calculating exposures by offsetting long *vs* short positions in any one currency.

Non-transactional FX risks

- *Translation risk* happens when FX variations affect an MNE's conversion of foreign assets or liabilities into its home currency. This includes dividends repatriated to headquarters, foreign currency loans and the valuation of foreign assets.

- *Speculative risk.* MNEs are free to decide what percentage of their currency risk they want to offset and may reason that in-house treasury specialists are as competent at trading as the banking counterparts onto whom they currently offload their FX risk.
- *Economic risk* is encountered when long-term adverse currency trends mean that it is no longer possible for the MNE to operate profitably and/or competitively in the countries where it incurs assets or liabilities.

Note as well an indirect economic risk when a competitor gains advantage by producing in a country with a weakening currency or selling into a country with a strengthening currency.

Managing foreign exchange risk

When an MNE fears that an adverse currency movement will have lasting effects, reconfiguring its entire global value chain is a viable (albeit costly) option. Immediate exposures, on the other hand, tend to be dealt with through short-term financial hedging.

"Natural" hedging

The most strategic response for MNEs that continuously accumulate assets in a weak currency and/or liabilities in a strong currency is to change their overall configuration to even out these exposures. One natural hedge involves adding to their revenue base in a currency they are short, for instance by expanding sales in the countries where that currency is used. The other natural hedge involves increasing their cost base in a currency they are long, for instance by running operations or buying from suppliers in the countries where it is used. By going long against shorts and short against longs, they reduce their overall exposure. The problem, of course, is that all these FX-driven changes take time and are very costly (especially where FDI is involved).

Short-term financial hedging

Where MNEs have no long-term view on a currency's strength, they can offset any exposure they face by "hedging" it through the FX markets. This involves a new transaction creating new exposures diametrically opposed to the original FX risk. That way, if the worst-case scenario happens and damages the MNE's original "underlying" position, the loss will be offset by the profits from the hedge. Of course, if the FX market moves and the original exposure ends up making a windfall profit, it is the hedge that will lose money. In both cases, the MNE will have fixed its ultimate FX price the day it transacts the hedge, for as long as this cover lasts (see Figure 10.1).

Unlike long-term structural reconfigurations of an MNE's value chain, short-term hedges do not prevent initial exposures from reappearing once a hedge matures, with the possibility that the new hedge will be transacted at a worse rate. Moreover, recurring short-term hedges increase transaction costs because the market-maker with whom the MNE transacts always seeks remuneration for its willingness to accept the risk by buying at below-market and selling at above-market prices. Having said that, it is also possible that once one hedge matures, the next will be at a better rate. Above all, short-term financial hedges are quicker and cheaper than huge structural reconfigurations.

Since financial hedging reduces the short-term volatility of earnings, analysis here necessarily centres on the risk attitudes revealed through MNEs' different policies in this respect. Some treat FX as a simple cost item and may be more willing to pay hedging-related transaction costs to reduce their risk. MNEs in this category are typified by their greater aversion to earnings volatility and by the fact that they define their role more narrowly as simply making and selling the products they

	Step 1. Underlying UK exporter long € Risk = € falls vs. £	Step 2. Hedge Hence new deal shorting (selling) € to offset long	Net effect of hedge
Scenario a. € then falls…	Underlying loss (-)	Hedge makes money (+)	0: profit offsets loss
Scenario b. € then rises…	"Windfall" profit (+)	Hedge loses money (-)	0: loss offsets profit

Hedging a long position

	Step 1. Underlying UK importer short € Risk = € rises vs. £	Step 2. Hedge Hence new deal long (buying) € to offset short	Net effect of hedge
Scenario a. € then rises…	Underlying loss (-)	Hedge makes money (+)	0: profit offsets loss
Scenario b. € then falls…	"Windfall" profit (+)	Hedge loses money (-)	0: loss offsets profit

Hedging a short position

Figure 10.1 MNE FX hedging.

offer. However, there are other MNEs who treat FX as a profit source and prefer to maintain some risks unhedged. This reflects both their willingness to assume different kinds of international risk – including FX-related – as well as their confidence that they can predict future currency market movements. This confidence tends to be based on either a short-term "technical" reading of market sentiment (using charts to estimate whether traders are optimistic "bulls" or pessimistic "bears") or else on longer-term "fundamental analysis" assessing the fair value of a currency based on indicators such as purchasing power parity or else macro-economic aggregates like inflation, growth and the trade balance.

Multinational treasury

MNE treasurers have an extremely broad remit, including investment planning, simulation, budgeting, management control, accounting, reporting, cash management, insurance and tax management. But probably the most important job they have is securing the capital that is the life blood of their company's operations.

External funding

Where the capital that an MNE generates through its internal operations does not suffice, it will need external sources. There are two main categories.

Debt finance

Few banks offer a full spectrum of debt instruments; the big players will all offer the main international banking products but as non-resident institutions may not be allowed to transact certain instruments in tightly controlled regimes. For this reason, MNEs tend to work with shortlists of global banks plus a few locals offering specific national services and information.

Finance's traditional "transformation" model sees savers deposit short-term funds with banks who then lend the funds back out to borrowers, usually for longer periods of time. In this model – which still functions, particularly for SMEs deemed too small to issue securities – providers and users of capital are mediated via banks, whose gross margins are comprised of the difference between the interest paid on deposits and the interest received on loans.

Back in the 1980s, however, solvency fears associated with this traditional model led to an international agreement that banks needed to reduce their risks. One way was to reduce their direct lending activities and start working as "lead managers" paid to support borrowers issuing securities directly to investors, who would then assume any default risk. This explains why today's MNEs acquire a much greater percentage of their debt funding from non-bank sources and why international financial market volumes have exploded over the past 40 years.

Investors decide whether to purchase debt issued by a given MNE based on their assessment whether the interest it offers constitutes a true reflection of its solvency. Corporate borrowers must generally pay a "risk premium" above and beyond the interest charged to a zero-risk borrower (usually the government). The more investors worry about an MNE's ability to repay debt, the greater the risk premium they require. As a result, a big part of a treasurer's job involves monitoring factors like public perception of an MNE's creditworthiness (often influenced by reports published by ratings agencies such as Standard & Poor's or Moody's) and the impact on investor psychology worldwide. Otherwise, under normal circumstances risk premiums tend to be higher the longer an MNE wants to borrow money – with the cost then depending on the difference between short- and long-term interest rates (called the "yield curve").

To increase their chances of borrowing cheaply, MNEs can either try to borrow in the short-term money markets – at rates often indexed to the London Interbank Offered Rate, known as Libor – or issue long-term debt securities like bonds, often in offshore "Euro" markets operating outside of national authorities' jurisdictions. Euromarkets tend to offer tax advantages as well as lower transaction costs. Above all, they are one way to access foreign investors who may not be active in an MNE's home market.

Even so, national financial markets remain very important to MNE funding, if only because many providers of capital, often "institutional" investors,are obliged by their statutes of incorporation to only purchase securities in the domestic capital market where they are familiar with the rules of disclosure. Hence most MNEs' interest to list their securities (both bonds and shares) on numerous exchanges worldwide. In turn, this raises questions about which unit within an MNE's configuration should be the entity signing a debt agreement. MNEs would prefer that one of their smaller units play this role and/or offer any requisite guarantee, if only to "ring-fence" potential default risk. Investors, on the other hand, prefer if their loans were backed by the assets of the MNE's larger, better capitalised entities.

Equity finance

The second external source of MNE funding is equity capital. Here investors purchase shares in the hope that values will rise. Price changes not only reflect general economic conditions but also expectations of a company's future profitability, which in itself is influenced by many factors.

One is the extent to which a company tries to increase its return on equity (ROE) by decreasing the proportion of its total funding that comes from equity rather than debt finance. If things go well, shareholders increase ROE using borrowed money. If things turn sour, the company must still reimburse its debt, increasing the risk of bankruptcy. "Leveraging" in this way is a high-risk/high-reward strategy. One interesting topic in MNE finance is the international variation in companies' attitudes towards this kind of "gearing" dilemma.

A second focus in international equity finance is the distinction between "passive" and "active" investment. The former often involves institutional investors eschewing any direct role in a company's management and simply seeking high returns (either over the long term or, if they are speculative "hedge funds", very rapidly). This differs from active investors who engage in operational and strategic decision-making..

MNEs often organise global "road shows" to convince investors worldwide of their shares' attractiveness. By so doing, they are trying to diversify their pool of potential funding sources. The question then becomes how any ensuing deals are to be organised. This will depend in turn on the kind of equity finance involved. Large MNEs seeking new equity often have few problems satisfying the procedural conditions required to get themselves listed on different national stock exchanges. SMEs seeking overseas equity finance face a challenge however. Because most major stock exchanges only list companies exceeding certain size and age thresholds, other equity finance mechanisms have had to be developed. One has been the rise of smaller stock exchanges (like Nasdaq in the United States or AIM in the UK) specifically geared towards smaller companies. Also worth noting is the rise of "private equity" arrangements where investors' equity stakes do not materialise in any tradable securities but simply enact changes in the company's ownership. One variant of this form of equity funding – "venture capital" – is interesting because of many countries' attempts to imitate the success that California's Silicon Valley had funding hi-tech start-ups in this way. Multinational finance can only be accurately understood in the context of the real international business strategies with which it is associated.

Internal funding sources

Many responsibilities vested with MNE finance officers means that treasury usually is the department with the greatest understanding of a group's consolidated financial flows. Given the specialist role assigned to most MNE subsidiaries nowadays, units' cash positions tend to be uneven, spread between units that are long cash (who have more than they need) and short ones. Addressing these imbalances often turns MNE treasurers into bankers to their own group.

Netting

Like the FX markets, banks usually price loan transactions with a bid-offer spread, paying less for deposits they receive than the interest they charge on loans they make. Thus, every time a company transacts with a bank, it incurs frictional costs. This makes it interesting to transact as few external deals as possible. Towards this end, many MNEs have created "netting" services that recycle some subsidiaries' surplus cash to fund others' deficits (see Figure 10.2). As is the case with all intra-MNE capital movements, the price that one unit pays its sister unit affects the profits or losses that a group declares in different geographic locations.

To perform this "clearing" function, MNE treasurers assess each subsidiary's current and future cash positions. For firms running global operations, analysis of this kind requires a very high-performance information system. Indeed, with their trading systems, spreadsheets, cash-flow simulations and economic studies, MNE treasury departments often resemble bank trading rooms. To support performance, many will centralise their most strategic treasury operations in a regional if not global centre. Tellingly, these centres are often located in jurisdictions that also offer MNEs' internal flows a favourable tax treatment.

Transfer pricing and tax implications

MNEs' intra-firm trading covers a variety of assets: tangible items like raw materials, parts and finished goods, but also capital or intangible items like loans, fees, royalties, trademarks and dividends. MNEs must price all these exchanges because they trade value from one international site to another. This makes transfer pricing a topic of great strategic importance.

Although international standards vary, most international authorities want transfer prices calculated on an objective "arm's length" basis, with MNEs pricing intra-firm flows as if the entities involved were

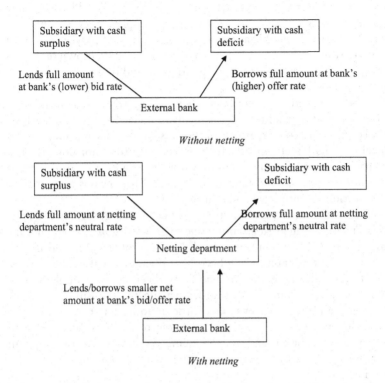

Figure 10.2 Netting reduces the costs associated with external funding operations.

unrelated. Examples of more objective transfer price categories might include:

- "cost plus pricing": where a defined margin is added to the return price of an item, often a finished product
- "cost pricing": where an item is transferred without any mark-up
- "profit split pricing": where subsidiaries split the ultimate operating profit realised on an item after it is sold by measuring the contribution that each has made.

Applying these precepts can be difficult, however, especially where an item is specific to one MNE (as if often the case with intermediary goods), meaning that no external market price exists for it. At that point, MNEs have other thoughts in mind when determining intra-firm transfer prices. The first is performance assessment. Transferring assets at a high price favours the unit making the transfer, whereas transfers made at a lower price favour the recipient. To address the inevitable conflicts arising from intra-unit transfer price negotiations, some MNEs engage in double accounting, quantifying employees' contributions to sister units to motivate them to see beyond their own team's bonus pool. Interdepartmental competition up and down the value chain is ferocious in many MNEs.

MNEs' second main concern when pricing transfers is minimising tax. In pure financial terms, it is in shareholders' interest to see losses declared in high-tax regimes and profits in low-tax regimes. At one level, MNEs benefit greatly from arbitraging the enormous international variation in corporation and other tax rates. Of course, avoiding (much less evading) tax in this way also has serious non-financial implications – both legal and ethical.

Tax behaviour is a key component of corporate governance, a broad concept attracting great attention due to growing concerns about transparency in MNE accounting. In the absence of credible and harmonised accounting standards, it becomes difficult to analyse the integrity of an MNE's fiscal behaviour. There have been many examples of large MNEs taking advantage of transfer pricing mechanisms, accounting loopholes and/or tax havens to pay little or nothing in tax. Many voices have denounced such practices and associated MNEs' financial management with their brand image – being yet another reason why multinational treasury functions cannot be analysed separately from other operations.

Bibliography

Arnold, G. (2015), *FT Guide to Bond and Money Markets*, FT Publishing International.

Association of Corporate Treasurers (updated continuously), *The Treasurer Digital Edition*, https://www.treasurers.org/thetreasurer/digitalarchive

Crabb, P. (2002), "Multinational Corporations and Hedging Exchange Rate Exposure", *International Review of Economics and Finance*, 11, 3, 299–314, December.

Euromoney (website updated continuously), https://www.euromoney.com/

Rugman, A. and Eden, L. (eds) (2017), *Multinationals and Transfer Pricing*, Routledge.

"So which one do you want to try first?"

11 International talent management

Essential summary

The world is VUCA (Volatile, Uncertain, Complex, and Ambiguous). Coined in the late 1980s, this trendy acronym emphasises the continuous, fast-paced, and disruptive changes that people and organisations face. It is widely accepted that people are a key resource to use in sustaining a competitive advantage in organisations. Indeed, the vast majority of CEOs consider attracting, managing and retaining talented people to be their main priority. In this context, the question becomes how Human Resources Management (HRM) can help a firm extend its global reach and market penetration while attracting, developing and retaining the best talent. Alongside marketing, finance and operations, international HRM is a strategic function focused on the management of a geographically dispersed workforce that needs to be marshalled to contribute to a company's successful internationalisation. This chapter explores some key challenges faced by MNEs in managing people internationally.

Global trends impacting MNEs' HRM needs

Since the 1990s, MNE HR managers have focused on identifying and managing those individuals who are capable of contributing disproportionately to their MNE's success. Interest in international talent management has increased dramatically in the past decade as organisations operate in an increasingly globalised world. There are four major trends in this area, impacting how MNEs manage their human resources internationally and explaining their growing interest in talent management.

Talent shortages

First, MNEs are all facing talent shortages, especially for highly skilled and pivotal positions in their foreign subsidiaries. One notable example is the on-going competition to recruit and retain talented employees in Chinese MNEs, where managerial staff turnover averages 40%. There is also a distinct shortfall in the availability of human talent capable of undertaking the increasingly technical reorganisations and product delivery system challenges facing numerous MNEs seeking to rebuild in the wake of the COVID-19 pandemic – with political barriers like immigration controls impeding the international movement of qualified technicians to companies in those countries where their talents are sorely needed. All these factors emphasise the role of HRM in implementing processes that support leadership development and career opportunities, thereby retaining valuable players in organisations.

Global talent war

The competition for talent plays out at more of a global level than a regional or national one. Managers no longer follow a traditional career path where they move up the career ladder in a single organisation. They are more likely to opt for a boundaryless and protean type of career, defined as one that spans a set of different organisations, sectors and countries. This modern attitude towards careers and employment relationships highlights individuals' role in defining their own career paths. Hence the increasing number of global talent and leadership development programmes that MNEs offer nowadays.

Demographics

The global job market is influenced by demographic factors such as increased life expectancy and the supply and flow of labour at the international level. As a result of globalisation and notwithstanding a number of recently imposed migration barriers, mobility has dramatically increased across geographical and cultural boundaries. The so-called "brain drain" phenomenon highlights new trends in the emigration of highly skilled workers from poor Global South countries to the Global North. In response, some governments have implemented macro-talent measures to attract expatriates back to the domestic job market. The end result sees MNEs and governments competing fiercely for the same global talent pool.

Rise of global hubs and cities

Another major trend shaping the management of people in MNEs is rapid urbanisation worldwide. Recent studies by consulting firms such as PWC have found that upwards of 1.5 million people are added to the world's urban population every week – with 50% of the global GDP being generated in only 300 metropolitan areas. This has led to the rise of global hubs, such as Silicon Valley in the USA, a key cluster for high-tech and digital companies. The Global Talent Competitiveness Index ranks the most attractive countries and cities based on opportunities for talent growth, entrepreneurial openness, social economic policies and innovation. In 2019, the top ten cities included Washington D.C., Copenhagen, Oslo, Vienna, Zurich, Boston, Helsinki, New York, Paris, and Seoul. These mega-cities and expert hubs attract talented people, who pursue career opportunities at the best specialised companies in their sector in the city where they have decided to live. To remain competitive and innovative, MNEs must therefore also learn how to manage the expectations of a workforce that has become increasingly demanding.

Institutions and resources

HRM strategy and practices are underpinned by two main concepts: the resource-based view; and the institution-based view. When applied in an international business environment, these two approaches can shed light on the management of people in MNEs.

The resource-based view

The resource-based view sees the firm as a unique combination of tangible and intangible resources, with human capital deemed to be a key factor of organisational success. This is best visualised using the Valuable, Rare, Difficult to imitate, and Organised (VRIO) framework delineated in Chapter 5 (see Table 11.1).

The institution-based view

When deployed at the international level, HR employee recruitment, training and development practices are significantly impacted by local rules, laws, and practices in the environments where the firm operates.

Table 11.1 VRIO Framework Applied to International HRM

Valuable	Do HR practices add value?	Training adds value as it improves the performance of an individual by 20%.
Rare	Are HR practices rare?	Some companies endeavour to adopt best HR practices that may, in turn, be perceived as valuable but not rare. 75% of UK organisations use coaching, for instance, which is therefore valuable but not rare.
Imitable	How imitable are human resources?	Specific skills can be learned through training, although complex capabilities, knowledge, and know-how acquired by a team through experience are more difficult to replicate however.
Organised	Is the firm organised to leverage its human resources and capabilities?	An MNE must adopt adequate management systems, processes, policies and organisational structures and a culture supporting local and global success.

Formal aspects

MNE subsidiaries must comply with and adapt to a host country's rules, laws, and regulations, first and foremost being employment law. For example, American HR managers operating in France or Germany may be disconcerted by the legal framework protecting employees in cases of redundancy or the closure of factories. Of course, this creates opportunities for placement companies, like the American MNE Manpower, that specialise in filling MNEs' human resource gaps. Against all odds, France has become Manpower's largest international market due to the country's increasing need for a flexible workforce.

Another formal institution is the educational system. Each country develops specific qualifications which emphasise certain managerial skills and attributes. Japanese managers, for instance, are expected to provide expertise and functional knowledge to their team – being core elements in the Japanese educational system. The end result is that differences in educational systems may translate into a high variability of managerial skills and profiles.

The same applies to language education, which is an important asset for international managers. Yet its provision differs greatly throughout the world, with recent reports indicating infinitely higher modern foreign language learning in European schools as opposed to their American counterparts. These differences imply that transferring skills and management practices across borders may prove ineffective. Quite the contrary, ideal HR practices in one country may be unproductive in another.

Informal aspects

The culture, values, and norms of a host country also create an informal set of rules that influence HR practices. As a result, staff selection and recruitment often follows different norms internationally. European MNEs, for example, tend to recruit locals or employees from a third country to manage their foreign subsidiaries, whereas Japanese firms, for historical and cultural reasons, are more likely to hire a Japanese manager for such roles. Conversely, the shortage of international managers in fast-growing countries such as China may require a firm to seek the right person on the global job market.

MNEs' diverse HRM practices

Another major challenge and priority concern for MNEs is selecting, motivating and rewarding their best employees to drive company performance. Two main types of employees work in MNEs: Host-Country Nationals (HCNs), commonly referred to as "locals"; and expatriates or other individuals living and working in a country other than their own. A further distinction can also be made between two types of expatriates: Parent-Country Nationals (PCNs) who are from the firm's parent (home) country but work in one of its foreign subsidiaries; and Third-Country Nationals (TCNs) who come from countries other than the home or host country.

In the 1980s and 1990s, MNEs often employed PCNs to control overseas operations from their headquarters and sent their most qualified people to foreign subsidiaries. Indeed, expatriates may play a pivotal role in the management of foreign operations as strategists, managers, ambassadors and representatives of the headquarters' interests. However, expatriate failure rates are high. This is due to the complexity of managerial responsibilities overseas, combined with the difficulties faced by families when adjusting to life in a foreign country. Nowadays, HCNs are increasingly recruited to participate and manage foreign operations, which has had a negative effect on expatriates' influence and the roles they are asked to perform. In short, MNEs make critical choices when recruiting and positioning managers in pivotal roles abroad. These often reflects an MNE's strategic posture vis-a-vis internationalisation itself.

There are three main approaches to hiring employees and filling top positions in overseas subsidiaries: ethnocentric, polycentric, and geocentric.

Ethnocentric hiring

The ethnocentric approach gives precedence to the norms and practices of the home (or parent) country of the company. Here, MNEs recruit and develop people from their home country and rely on PNCs.

Polycentric hiring

Conversely, the polycentric approach emphasises the norms and culture of the host country. Here MNEs recruit local nationals to avoid language and cultural barriers.

Geocentric hiring

Alternatively, MNEs may adopt a geocentric approach whereby the most suitable managers are recruited regardless of their nationality. Hence, top managers overseas are selected as the best people for a position and may be PCNs, HCNs or TCNs. This approach can support geographically dispersed MNEs in the creation of a global corporate culture.

Global talent management

Global talent management encompasses all organisational activities that aim to attract, select, develop and retain talented employees in firms operating across borders. The specificity of talent management, compared to HRM, is employee segmentation, with pivotal positions in the organisation being reserved for people capable of making a disproportionate contribution to the company's competitive advantage. The COVID-19 pandemic has shaken up work practices, forcing many staff members (including in the HRM function) to work remotely. The added costs, along with a revenue squeeze, meant many MNEs would find themselves implementing a hiring freeze. In this highly unpredictable and disruptive environment, MNEs focus on maintaining the flow of talent, ideas and innovation. This implies upskilling or reskilling employees locally and tapping into the company's talent pool internationally to nurture capacity, capability and agility.

Like all international business functions, global talent management (in the wider sense) and HRM (in the narrower sense) involve micro-level MNE strategies unfolding in a context defined by macro-level international constraints.

Attracting global talent

Among the best practices developed by MNEs seeking to recruit the best people, three main approaches can be outlined. First, a clear employee value proposition establishes what the company will offer in terms of leadership development and career growth. It can be communicated through advertisements, job descriptions, websites and organisational social media. However, if this proposition is perceived as unclear or inconsistent or is poorly communicated, it may deter prospective talent from joining the organisation.

Secondly, it is of prime importance that MNEs develop a global talent management strategy consistent with its organisational strategy, mission, values and culture. If the MNEs' actions do not match their discourse, this may lead to public mistrust and consequently damage the firm's reputation as an employer of choice for talent.

Thirdly, the culture fit between the employee and the company must be considered during the recruitment process. A study conducted in 2015 by the Society of Human Resource Management claims that when individual and organisational values diverge, it may cost the organisation up to 60% of the person's annual salary. Hence, MNEs need to clarify what they stand for and select the right talent for fruitful collaboration.

A useful example at this level is a recruitment strategy developed by the Chinese MNE Alibaba. In 2016, an innovative recruitment and training scheme called Alibaba Global Leadership Academy was launched in order to internationalise the company's workforce, which is predominantly Chinese, and help it to develop a global mindset. The scheme aims to attract talent from major foreign markets targeted by the firm as part of its internationalisation strategy. It includes on-the-job training and a 16-month cultural immersion at headquarters, located in Hangzhou, China. Ultimately, this initiative helps nurture future Alibaba global leaders who will bridge the gap between China and the rest of the world.

Developing talent

The development of global talent has been at the forefront of MNE for a long time. Among the talent management practices taking place in large organisations, coaching and mentoring are often identified as the most effective. Coaching is used in big companies for performance, leadership and career development purposes. Typically, leaders are offered coaching support when they transition between roles, face the prospect of promotion or join a talent management scheme. Talent development activities and leadership coaching used to be the prerogative of top managers and executives. However, mentoring schemes, whereby a senior manager is paired with a less experienced employee, are particularly valued by younger generations.

With millennials comprising over 50% of the global workforce, recent studies have discovered a growing tendency among MNEs to design talent development programmes for graduates and junior and middle managers identified as having high potential. Among the various practices used to develop leadership capabilities and enhance employee performance, coaching and mentoring help extend the network of talented employees, raise awareness of organisational politics and foster intercultural competence. These are essential aids for a fast-track career in an MNE.

Retaining talent

Rewards, promotion and career progression are an important set of HR policies used to recognise and retain the contributions of talented staff. Employees identified as high performers (or possessing high potential) are often positioned in an MNE's talent pool for succession planning and leadership development purposes. Typically, a talented employee would benefit from developmental activities, such as short-term international assignments, shadowing, coaching, mentoring and training. Rewarding talent may also be achieved by providing exclusive perks in the form of discounts and access to healthcare, and sport facilities. MNEs are increasingly outsourcing these services to third-party organisations (e.g. Perks at Work), which provide a differentiated offer to talented employees.

In sum, people are a key asset for global performance and organisational competitiveness. Global talent management and human resource practices must constantly be adjusted to support a firm's internationalisation strategy and reflect societal changes in the countries where it operates.

Bibliography

INSEAD (2019), *The Global Talent Competitiveness Index 2019*, Fontainebleau.

Minocha, S. and Hristov, D. (2019), *Global Talent Management: An Integrated Approach*, Sage: London.

Scullion, H., Collings, D. G. and Caligiuri, P. (2010) "Global Talent Management", *Journal of World Business*, Volume 45, No. 2, pp. 105–108.

Sparrow, P., Brewster, C. and Harris, H. (2017) *Globalizing Human Resource Management*, Routledge: Abingdon (2nd edition).

"The world certainly is getting smaller".

12 The future of international business

Essential summary

Given the incredibly diverse circumstances in which they operate, MNEs find they must always keep an eye on future trends, often employing qualified staff to detect and plan for political, economic, social, technological and/or ecological patterns that could have a significant impact on their operations. This "competitive intelligence" function aims to help companies position themselves to take advantage of future opportunities while gaining protection from possible adversity.

Ascertaining trends' relative significance can be difficult, however – especially when it is unfamiliar foreign environments that are being scanned. In response, the McKinsey consultancy group has long been surveying international business practitioners to get their opinions regarding which trends are most likely to have the greatest effect on MNEs' environments and operations. Two of the phenomena that regularly come at the top of the list – the emergence of the Global South and technology's impact on international business – form the basis of this final chapter. The third – the growing importance of green business – is the topic of another mini-textbook in this Routledge "Essentials" series.

The changing geography of international business

It is important to note that notwithstanding the economic emergence of the Global South – as evidenced by these countries' higher GDP growth rates and rising proportion of global trade and FDI – the world's older industrialised nations (the "Global North") retain technological, institutional and financial resources that continue to serve them well. At the same time, there is little doubt that the arrival of new power-houses constitutes a sea change in international business, and one well worth exploring in detail.

"Global South" is a vague term referring to countries with very different back stories and prospects. The best-known classifications, famously formulated by ex-Goldman Sachs economist Jim O'Neill, have been the BRICs (Brazil, Russia, India and China) plus the CIVETs (Colombia, Indonesia, Vietnam, Egypt, Turkey and South Africa). Other emerging economies include Malaysia, Mexico, Nigeria and Thailand – not to mention Eastern Europe's "transition" ex-communist regimes. Reflecting this diversity, MNE managers need a differentiated understanding of each Global South market in which they operate. Strategies will vary depending on whether the country is envisioned as a manufacturing platform, consumer market, the birthplace of new rivals or a combination thereof. The sequencing of these three stages typifies much of the Global South's emergence and offers a logical way of structuring analysis in this area.

New manufacturing powerhouses

Growth in the Global South can be divided between "endogenous" (or internal) dynamics (best theorised by Nobel laureate Kenneth Arrow) and "exogenous" (or external) drivers. The latter category includes FDI by foreign firms that use these locations as production platforms for products that until recently were often re-exported back to the Global North. Much has been written about the main drivers for FDI in the Global South –currently totalling ca. $700 billion annually and accounting for of 50% of all global FDI nowadays, nearly twice as much as just one decade ago. Analysis usually starts with the generally (much) lower labour costs in this part of the world. But there are other factors as well explaining these countries' rise as manufacturing powerhouses. One is the enormous number of young Global South engineers and scientists currently being trained to the highest standards. Economists like Paul Krugman have now dismissed the old idea that the world's emerging economies are destined to specialise in low value-added production. Instead, they have broadened the number of sectors where the Global South's advantages play out. Earlier problems with communications or infrastructure are increasingly being resolved, with countries "leapfrogging" historical stages of technological development. Otherwise, the rapid growth that many Global South economies are experiencing as consumer markets also supports their further attractiveness as manufacturing centres. Given sentiments of "economic patriotism" typifying some Global South consumers (much like many of their Global North counterparts), MNEs know they can earn their new customers' good will if they achieve "insiderisation" status by producing locally. In the Global South like elsewhere, MNEs derive an advantage from reducing perceptions of foreignness.

This does not mean that there are no limits to the tide of Global South manufacturing FDI. Operating conditions in these environments can be very different from what MNEs are used to elsewhere. Indeed, they are often much more difficult. Levels of corruption are demonstrably higher in the Global South; supply chains can be harder to coordinate; "institutional voids" can create great uncertainty about financial, legal and regulatory conditions; and notwithstanding China's enormous "Belt and Road" initiative, logistics infrastructure remains subpar in many places. The ability to manage these "non-market factors" requires specific competencies that may not always be widely available throughout all MNEs. It remains that many managers are willing to take on these challenges nowadays, largely because of their desire to penetrate fast growing new markets. It is a general consensus about the future of international business – albeit one that should be measured, however, against a concurrent rise in pessimism alternatively as attributed to "slowbalisation" (globalisation's slowdown in recent years) and the terrible COVID-19 crisis afflicting the planet since early 2020.

Selling into the Global South

Rising wages in many Global South countries has led to rapid expansion in the size of their middle classes. Moreover, many informed optimists like development specialist Jeffrey Sachs expect this to continue – with bodies like the OECD predicting that Asia alone will account for two-thirds of the global middle-class population by the year 2030. Numerous MNEs, especially ones whose existing markets are saturated, monitor the trend in the hope that it means solvent new consumer demand for their goods and services. In all likelihood, emerging market citizens' average per-capita income will remain lower than their Global North counterparts for years to come. But the sheer size of the populations involved makes downstream market entry here an attractive proposition for many MNEs.

The expansion of Global South middle classes is also significant because of the kinds of products that households purchase when they shift out of poverty. According to Abraham Maslow's famous pyramid, as income rises people tend to spend more on non-essential items (consumer durables, mobility, leisure) that were once beyond their reach. This is a great opportunity for firms in the sectors concerned. Note an analytical distinction that can be made at this level between markets experiencing their "first equipment" and "product renewal" stages. The latter concept mainly applies in older, more established markets where consumers only purchase products once existing goods become obsolescent. The former involves products being diffused for the first time – and therefore entailing much greater volumes. It is the situation arising in many emerging economies today.

Selling in the Global South can be very costly, however, if only because enormous variations between these national markets often require major adaptations. Explanations for this variability can be cultural in nature and/or reflect huge disparities in purchasing power, divided between a few affluent citizens who have achieved a comfortable standard of living and vast numbers of "bottom-of-the-pyramid" consumers whose purchasing power remains limited. To address this latter population – which is numerically much greater – MNEs are increasingly develop "frugal" products that are cheaper and/or offer lesser functionalities than the variants sold elsewhere. In turn, this intimates that they adapt their production processes to new constraints – always a costly proposition.

The question is whether this adaptation of an MNE's product range is worth the expense. With their much higher cost bases and despite all their cost-saving outsourcing and FDI initiatives, many Global North MNEs struggle to turn a profit selling at minimal so-called China prices. Companies originating in the Global South, on the other hand, are more accustomed to environments characterised by low costs, low prices and (sometimes) lower quality. This gives them a competitive advantage in some of the international business battles that are likely to be waged in the future.

Global South MNEs as new players on the world stage

Most Global South MNEs have yet to become household names in the Global North, but this is already changing (see Figure 12.1) as their competitive advantages – starting with lower return costs – begin to play out. The question then becomes to what extent the international business environment will remain conducive to these companies catching up with their Global North counterparts.

Global South multinationals have strengths that are particularly advantageous in their home markets, where attitudes towards foreignness can be quite complicated. It is true that real attraction exists in many

Sector Country	Primary	Industrial	High-tech
Brazil	Petrobras (oil) Vale (mining)	Braskem (petrochemicals) WEG (motors)	Embraer (aerospace) Oi (telecoms)
Russia	Gazprom (gas) Lukoil (oil)	Avtovaz (automotive) Evraz (metallurgy)	Rostec (engineering) RSCC (satellites)
India	Reliance (energy, materials) ArcelorMittal (steel)	Tata (automotive) Bharti Airtel (telecom)	Ranbaxy (pharmaceuticals) Infosys (software)
China	Sinopec (oil) Baoshan Iron and Steel (metals)	Haier (appliances) Chery (automotive)	Lenovo (computing) Huawei (telecoms)

Figure 12.1 Sample of BRICs-born MNEs joining the global elite.

emerging economies for foreign products associated until recently with a lifestyle and standard of living that few consumers could attain. Indeed, there are a number of sectors – luxury, for instance – where several MNEs only thrive because new Global South customers offset the saturation of their traditional markets. At the same time, this one example only looks at a small "top-of-the-pyramid" population. For the vast majority of Global South consumers seeking to purchase non-luxury items, studies have regularly shown that an ongoing fascination with Global North brands is offset by strong country-of-origin preferences benefiting local companies with which they are familiar.

MNEs from the Global South are aware of this effect and have mobilised it to create business models that they hope will be just as applicable in the Global North as in their countries of origin – an optimism supported in research conducted by specialist academics such as Columbia University's Karl Sauvant. One famous example of this sea change in MNE behaviour is the "Indian way of doing business", being the title of a best-selling book highlighting the cultural practices of companies originating in South Asia whose corporate culture of solidarity has stood them in good stead as they moved onto the world stage. Whereas North–North and North–South FDI flows dominated international business throughout the 20th century, in recent years an increasing proportion of foreign direct investment has involved South–South and even South–North flows. The end result is a network of global exchanges that will be much more multi-polar than ever before. The implications for MNEs' power and location decisions are enormous.

Artificial intelligence's impact on international business

The Fourth Industrial Revolution will dramatically change the way people live, work and connect with one another around the world. Unprecedented technological advances are redefining human activities and even question what it means to be human in the 21st century. The last decade has witnessed incredible advances in artificial intelligence (AI). From the automation of production lines to driverless cars, these technological innovations contribute to increased economic growth and create major shifts in the way firms operate both domestically and internationally.

The *Encyclopaedia Britannica* defines AI as "the ability of a digital computer or computer-controlled robot to perform tasks commonly associated with intelligent beings". Such tasks include reasoning, discovering meaning, generalising and learning from past experience. The term "machine learning" refers to digital systems' ability to use the data derived from these intellectual processes to predict what customers want and deliver that information quickly.

In international business, data analytics and translation services are already reducing cross-border barriers to trade. It remains that AI's further development in this area still faces a number of challenges. Neither utopia nor dystopia, AI is likely to resolve certain problems but also create new ones relating to social inequality, MNE configurations, data privacy, global governance and human resources.

Economic growth

Insofar as AI's development boosts productivity, it is likely to have a positive impact on economic growth and therefore create new cross-border trade opportunities. The problem is that countries may not reap AI's productive benefits in the short run because of the time it takes to leverage the benefits of the investments in training or in new and better business practices.

AI is also likely to affect economic growth by helping countries accelerate their transition into a service economy. Drawing on the VRIO framework (see Chapter 7), AI gives prominence to those skills that add production value (exemplified by the growing tendency towards embedding services into goods sold internationally). In this way, it helps to make global value chains more efficient. On the other hand, there is widespread worry about the rise of AI-induced unemployment, especially where low-skilled or traditional blue-collar manufacturing jobs are concerned. With AI as with so many other innovations affecting the future of international business, the disadvantages need to be analysed in conjunction with the benefits.

Global supply chains

AI helps MNEs manage supply chain risks by improving both warehouse inventory management and delivery accuracy in lean manufacturing regimes. Similarly, the deployment of the Internet of Things (IoT), which interconnects computers, materials, supplies and customers, enables production systems to self-regulate and thereby become more flexible in terms of their ability to meet market demand. IoT also further improves communication and maintenance up and down the supply chain, ensuring that production is more closely tailored to customer specifications – always a difficult proposition in international business.

At the same time, the arrival of suppliers with advanced capabilities in robotics, design and R&D could have a significant effect on MNEs' existing configurations. There is every chance that AI will partially reverse the offshoring and international outsourcing trends that have dominated international business for the past 30 or 40 years. This is because when automation and 3D-printing shape the production process, the negative aspects of having internationalised supply chains (including logistics, quality and control problems) become more apparent, especially where products reliant on low-cost labour and economies of scale are involved.

Cross-border digital trade

AI also enables SMEs to compete globally thanks to digital platforms like eBay, as well as digital translation services. This latter facility is particularly interesting because of its potential for driving demand by facilitating communications with all sorts of foreign language speakers. One example is the 17.5% increase in eBay's US exports to Spanish-speaking Latin-America Another was Google's 2018 announcement that its deep learning-based Neural Machine Translation (NMT) system could reduce translation errors by 55%–85% compared to the previous generation of Google Translate. In short, AI may support SMEs' internationalisation by reducing language barriers and enabling greater access to customers worldwide. At the same time, managers do need to remain aware of how crucial cultural awareness and language skills remain when conducting business internationally (see Chapter 5). Google Translate or NMT are not yet able to host a meeting with a Spanish executive or Indonesian partner.

Data and trade negotiations

Data has turned into a factor of prime importance in modern international businesses due to the economies of scale it generates. Statistical predictions from Google or Alibaba, for instance, improve with the quality and quantity of data available. By having access to more data, AI helps MNEs to discern potential variations in international customers' intent with greater accuracy. The same applies to analysis of large product, tariff and trade policy databases - exemplified by Brazil'sIntelligent Technology and Trade Initiative, which uses AI to improve trade negotiations by calculating different trade scenarios together with their economic impact.

Data alone does not give meaningful results, however. Instead, it is the the type of data (and accumulated searches from previous customers) that affects the quality of search results. The virtuous circle for data – reliant MNEs therefore starts with getting more customers to generate more data; improving in turn service quality; and using this improvement to further grow market share. The economies of scales achieved through this mechanism derive from positive direct network effects (also called network externalities) where the value of a service increases as the number of users rises. This is redolent at a technological level to the international business version of Granovetter's Network Theory (see Chapter 6), where clusters develop in large part because success breeds success.

Note that the AI model contrasts with existing trade theories since economies of scale are viewed here as being based on maximal exploitation of existing fixed costs and/or on maximum matching of market supply and demand. Traditional trade models are not particularly relevant to the world of AI, however. The emphasis here is on the nature of competition and access to data.

Global regulation of AI

Managing cross-border data flows intimates a need to subject this whole domain to regulations that are also global in nature. Customer privacy and data security have received enormous worldwide attention in recent years, with the so-called GAFA Big Tech MNEs

(Google, Apple, Facebook, and Amazon) all being closely scrutinised in different national jurisdictions for the way they collect and use personal data. Customers around the world seem to have become increasingly cautious about sharing private information and fear losing control over this asset. MNEs and other businesses, together with national and international institutions, are constantly under threat of seeing their information and data systems breached, potentially resulting in a fraudulent use of customer data. Hence the emergence of a number of data protection policies and regulations, with one leading example being the EU's General Data Protection Regulation (GDPR) protocol. Despite these steps, however, there is still a dearth of global regulation as regards the cross-border availability, anonymisation and circulation of data.

AI and international business practitioners

Developing a national workforce with AI skills has become a priority strategy for many policy-makers worldwide. Due to the global shortage of talent in this area, MNEs seeking competitive advantage have increasingly joined and sometimes even superseded these state initiatives in a bid to attract, develop and retain the kinds of talents who are capable of sharing the tacit knowledge and collaborative innovation with which AI is associated. Cities everywhere are devising public-private initiatives that they hope will turn them into AI hubs and global talent magnets. These investments can vary from vocational training and skills enhancement (with its STEM science, technology, engineering and mathematics focus) to the kind of life-long learning needed to help mature professionals adapt to digitally enhanced work and business practices.

It is crucial to remember that international business is ultimately not a quantitative discipline but instead a social science, with all this implies about mastering human beings' so-called softer skills set, starting with creativity, independence and dynamism. In the end, international business practitioners never really manage companies – they manage people. And that is a whole other business.

Bibliography

Cappelli, P. et al. (2010), *The India Way: How India's Top Managers Are Revolutionizing Management*, Harvard Business Press.

Meltzer, J. (13 December 2018), "The impact of artificial intelligence on international trade", *Brookings Institute*, available at https://www.brookings.edu/, accessed 25 June 2020

Ransbotham, S., Kiron, D., Gerbert, P. and Reeves, M. (2017), "Reshaping Business with Artificial Intelligence: Closing the Gap between Ambition and Action", *MIT Sloan Management Review*, 59(1), pp. n/a-0.

Sachs, J. (2005), *The End of Poverty: How We Can Make It Happen In Our Lifetime*, London: Penguin Books

Sauvant, K. et al. (eds) (2010), *Foreign Direct Investments from Emerging Markets*, Palgrave Macmillan.

Index

Printed in the United States
by Baker & Taylor Publisher Services

Printed in the United States
by Baker & Taylor Publisher Services